Grolier
16.50

Planetology

PLANETOLOGY

Comparing Other Worlds to Our Own

Fred Schaaf

A Venture Book

Franklin Watts
A Division of Grolier Publishing
New York • London • Hong Kong • Sydney
Danbury, Connecticut

Illustrations by Vantage Art, Inc.
Photographs ©: American Museum of Natural History: 26; Astronomy
Society of the Pacific: 24; The Bettmann Archive: 32, 41; Finley
Holiday Films: 76, 102, 112; Jet Propulsion Laboratory, NASA: 28,
104; Lick Observatory, University of California: 96; NASA: 22, 35,
37, 39, 43, 45, 53, 56, 61, 63, 74, 82, 93, 106; Photo Researachers:
14, 20, 108 (Julian Baum/SPL), 59 (NASA/Mark Marten/SS), 100
(NASA/SPL); Yerkes Observatory, University of Chicago: 18.

Library of Congress Cataloging-in-Publication Data

Schaaf, Fred
Planetology: comparing other worlds to our own/Fred Schaaf.
p.   cm.   (A Venture book)
Includes bibliographical references and index.
Summary: Discusses the planets, with particular emphasis on
comparing them to each other and especially to Earth.
ISBN 0-531-11300-0 (lib. bdg.)   ISBN 0-531-15828-4 (pbk.)
1. Planetology—Juvenile literature. [1. Planetology. 2. Planets.]
I. Title.
QB602.s3 1996
523.5—DC20   96-15826
                                                       CIP
                                                        AC

Contents

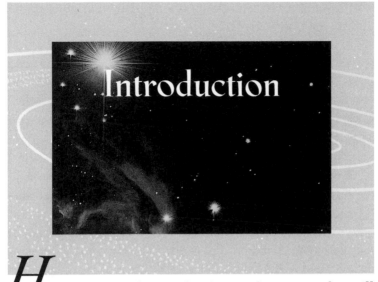

Introduction

*H*undreds, even thousands of years from now, what will people remember most about our time? If we completely ruin our beautiful planet with wars or pollution, that will be remembered most of all. But there's another possibility, a far happier one. The people alive a thousand years from now may look back and recall that ours was the time when humans first traveled to other worlds in space. The choice is ours to make.

I have a feeling that if we continue our plans to explore other worlds, we will also succeed in avoiding wars and protecting our environment. I say this because our quest to learn about other planets is also a quest to learn about our favorite, most precious planet—Earth. The most important idea of the science of planetology is that what we find out about other worlds can help us to better understand, appreciate, and love our own world.

Planetology—the Study of Worlds in Comparison

Imagine what it would be like if you only knew one person in your life, yourself—you had never met anybody else.

That is what it has been like for scientists to know just one planet, the planet Earth.

It is not just exciting and fun to meet new people. You notice the similarities and differences between you and them and end up learning more about who you are and who you want to be. In much the same way, learning about other worlds gives us examples for comparison and contrast to our Earth. We can also see what all worlds have in common and how all worlds work.

Actually, there is no one name for this important idea. Nor is there a single name for a branch of science that has this idea as its central principle. I have appropriated the term "planetology," which really just means the study of the planets and other condensed matter (moons, asteroids, comets, and meteoroids).

In recent years, many scientists have chosen to use the term "planetary science." Since there are so many different individual specialties involved in the study of the planets—meteorology, geology, chemistry, physics, and special combinations of all of them—scientists seem to have backed off from the idea that all these individual disciplines could work together toward one larger, well-defined goal. But I firmly believe we should reassert taking a larger view of planetary study. We should concentrate on comparing worlds, at least as a beginning of planetary studies. Whatever you choose to call the study of worlds in comparison, I hope you will find the chapters that follow not just exciting but also thought provoking.

You will probably learn more about the planets in the years ahead than science has learned in all of history. I hope that this book will prepare you to think creatively and wisely about the incredible planetary discoveries made during your lives.

C h a p t e r   O n e

Following the Wanderers

*B*efore we can study what space probes of recent years have discovered and make an in-depth comparison of the planets, we need to learn some of the more basic facts about the planets. How can we do this? We can retrace through history the steps that science took to slowly but steadily increase our knowledge of the planets.

For thousands of years, human beings have looked at the lights in the night sky with wonder and curiosity. Early observers noticed that most of the lights—the twinkling stars—do not change their positions in relation to each other. They always maintain the same patterns. The stars that form the Big Dipper or Leo the Lion maintain the same basic arrangement year after year.

These early watchers of the heavens also noticed something else. They noticed that a few of the brightest points of light in the night sky shined more steadily than the twinkling stars. They also noticed something even more strange and wondrous: these bright, untwinkling lights changed their positions among the stars. Although some moved more slowly than others, all of these special objects moved from night to night, week to week, year to year.

The ancient Greeks had a name for these special lights. They called them the *planetai*, which means "the wanderers." Today, of course, we refer to them as the *planets*.

Planets in the Zodiac

Ancient humans kept track of the planets' behavior mostly because they feared that these strange moving lights might influence human affairs. The earliest sky watchers must have thought that the planets were powerful magic spirits or supernatural beings.

Even the culture that produced the first scientists, the Greeks, named the planets after their traditional gods and goddesses. The Romans followed their example. The Romans called the most consistently visible and stately planet Jupiter (the name of their king of the gods). They called the brightest and most beautiful planet Venus (the name of their goddess of love and beauty). The reddest and most variable planet was named Mars (after the Roman god of war).

The early scientific thinkers in Greece certainly did not believe that the planets were gods and goddesses or that the planets were influenced by such beings. They sought through some observation and much reasoning to figure out which planets were farthest away from Earth and what caused their peculiar motions. They also noticed that the planets (and the sun and moon, which could be regarded as very special forms of wanderers) could always be found in a band of constellations (star patterns). This band became known as the *zodiac*. The word zodiac is related to zoo and zoology, which is the study of animals. Originally all the constellations in the zodiac were named for animals.

The zodiac forms a circle around the heavens, and ancient astronomers noticed that as the sun, moon, and planets moved from one zodiac constellation to the next they eventually made the journey all the way around the circle. The moon takes only about one month to do so, while the sun, Mercury, and Venus each take about one year, Mars completes one circle in two years, Jupiter in about twelve, and Saturn in about thirty. Observers understood that that the longer a planet took to make this circle around the heavens, the farther it must be from the center of the circle.

The Ptolemaic System

The key question was: what is at the center of the system of the planets; what do they all circle around? The answer seemed obvious. The planets circle around the sky of our world. Earth must be at the center.

One famous Greek astronomer, Aristarchos of Samos (about 310–230 B.C.), had a different idea. He suggested that the planets, including Earth, orbit around the sun. Other Greek and Roman scientists believed in a *geocentric* (Earth-centered) system.

This dominant, but incorrect, belief was expressed most influentially by the Roman astronomer Claudius Ptolemaeus, better known as Ptolemy (about A.D. 120–190). As a result, the idea of an Earth-centered system is often called the *Ptolemaic system*.

Many of the ideas expressed in Ptolemy's work, *The Almagest*, guided scientific thinking throughout the Middle Ages. In other words, for a span of no less than about 1,300 years, people believed an idea that was wrong!

Part of the reason that the Ptolemaic system survived so long is that human beings tended to believe that they were so important that they must be at the physical center of

Roman astronomer Claudius Ptolemaeus,
better known as Ptolemy, was the strongest advocate
of the geocentric (Earth-centered) system.

things. The other reason it survived is that it worked pretty
well. By "worked" I mean that it was able to explain why
the planets went where they did, and even to do what any
good scientific theory ought to be able to do—predict. The
Ptolemaic system could predict where a planet would be in
the months or years ahead.

The catch was that to make the Ptolemaic system "work," it was necessary to make elaborate adjustments to the theory. A mark of a good scientific theory is a basic simplicity in its design. The Ptolemaic system was not simple at all. Furthermore, careful observation revealed that the planets had departed markedly from their predicted positions. There were two major problems that required adjustments to the theory: the basic motions of Mercury and Venus and the *retrograde motion* of the planets.

If the sun, Mercury, and Venus all circle the zodiac in about one year, which is closest to Earth? Which is farthest? Mercury and Venus have a peculiar habit, unlike any of the other planets, of never moving very far away from the sun in the sky. Neither planet ever rises more than a few hours before the sun or sets more than a few hours after the sun. Some thinkers began to believe that these two planets might actually circle the sun, while the sun circles Earth. If this were true, then not everything circled Earth.

In addition, the Ptolemaic system could not explain retrograde motion, an apparent reversing of a planet's normal direction of travel in relation to the background of stars. For a while each year (less often for Mars) each planet appears to stop, move backward (west rather than east) among the stars, stop again, and then resume its usual movement. To try to explain this phenomenon, scientists introduced more and more *epicycles*—circles for the planets to travel around while the circles themselves orbited Earth—to the Ptolemaic system.

Scientists now realize that retrograde motion is a simple effect of perspective, of our changing viewpoint as Earth goes through space. When Mars seems to stop and then move backward among the stars, it is like what you might experience when you pass a car on the highway.

Because Mars moves more slowly than Earth, it seems to drift backward just as a slower-moving car does when you view it against the background scenery.

People who believed in a geocentric system could never quite explain retrograde motion.

Copernicus, Kepler, and Galileo

As long as the Ptolemaic system was accepted, there could be no real thought that Earth was a planet itself, at least not a planet that could be compared to the other planets. For planetology and the comparison of worlds to really be born, several things had to happen. And the first was that the geocentric view of the Ptolemaic system had to be replaced with the correct, *heliocentric* (sun-centered) view.

The crucial challenge came at last in 1543, from the pen of a Polish astronomer who is best known by the Latinized form of his name: Nicholas Copernicus (1473–1543). Copernicus had the courage, the originality, and the clarity of vision to reject the accepted version of how the universe was ordered. The heliocentric system in which the planets circle the sun is still sometimes called the *Copernican system* in his honor.

This system was neither accepted nor even proven valid for decades after Copernicus's book was printed and distributed. It was German astronomer and mathematician Johannes Kepler (1571–1630) and Italian astronomer and physicist Galileo Galilei (1564–1642) who finally proved the validity of the heliocentric system.

Kepler was the assistant of the skilled Danish observational astronomer Tycho Brahe (1546–1601). Brahe's many years of careful measurements of star and planet positions gave Kepler, a mathematical genius, what he needed to prove that the Copernican system works.

The problem was that a heliocentric setup for the plan-

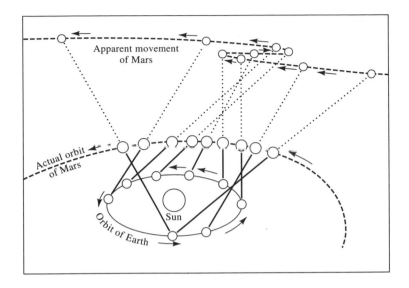

Because Mars and the other superior planets move more slowly than Earth, these planets occasionally appear to drift backward among the background of stars. This phenomenon—retrograde motion—is an illusion caused by our change in viewpoint as Earth moves through space.

ets did not accurately predict where the planets would be— if you assumed that the planets' orbits were circular. Kepler's calculations proved that the planets' orbits are not perfect circles. These more elongated paths are called *ellipses*.

Kepler's math would have begun to convince other scientists. But, as it turned out, observations made with a new invention—the telescope—also began to shake the old beliefs.

The most important early telescopic observations were made by Galileo. He may not have been quite the first to use a telescope for astronomical purposes, but he certainly used it effectively. More importantly, he was both able and willing to publish his support for the Copernican view of

Polish astronomer Nicholas Copernicus is credited
with envisioning the modern theory of a heliocentric
(sun-centered) system.

things. Beginning in 1609, his telescopic observations
revealed to him many marvels: mountains and craters on
the moon, spots on the sun, countless stars making up the
glow in the sky we know as the Milky Way.

His observations of Jupiter and Venus were most significant. He spotted four little "stars" near Jupiter. These Galilean satellites, which changed their positions in a matter of hours or even minutes and were clearly orbiting Jupiter, were actually the four biggest moons of Jupiter. They provided indisputable evidence that not everything revolved around Earth.

More telling yet were Galileo's observations of the phases of Venus. Not even the theory that Venus orbited the sun, which orbited Earth, was consistent with the progression of Venus's phases. Only a completely heliocentric arrangement could explain what he saw.

After Kepler and Galileo, the idea that we live in something that could justly be called a *solar system* (a system of the sun) slowly but surely came into acceptance. This opened the door to planetology, to the comparison of worlds, and to the consideration of Earth as a member of a whole family of worlds.

Terrestrial Planets and Gas Giants

Now that scientists understood how the planets are arranged, they began to classify them in interesting ways. For example, planets closer to the sun than Earth (inferior to Earth in distance from the sun) are called the *inferior planets*. Planets farther out from the sun than Earth (superior to Earth in distance from the sun) are called the *superior planets*. This distinction between worlds is based solely on their positions relative to Earth. These descriptions tell you little or nothing about the physical nature of the planets.

Another method of assigning the planets to groups speaks of them as belonging to either the inner solar system or the outer solar system. The dividing line between

Galileo's early experiments with the telescope eventually
yielded key observations of the moons of Jupiter, the
phases of Venus, and other sightings that helped
support the Copernican theory of the solar system.

the inner and outer solar system is the large gap between Mars and Jupiter (where the *asteroids* ramble). This grouping also tells you very little about the planets themselves. About all you know is that, if all else is equal, a planet in the outer solar system will be in a colder state than one in the inner solar system.

The most useful basic categories for planetologists are *terrestrial planet* and *Jovian planet*. "Terrestrial" means "of Earth" or "like Earth," while "Jovian" means "of Jupiter" or "like Jupiter." Mercury, Venus, Earth, and Mars are all terrestrial planets. Jupiter, Saturn, Uranus, and Neptune are all Jovian planets. (Where does that leave Pluto? In neither group, and as we will see, that may be an accurate appraisal of that strange planet.)

Much of what we now know about terrestrial planets and Jovian planets took hundreds of years of telescopic observation to discover. (Uranus, Neptune, and Pluto were not even identified until several centuries after Galileo lived.) What we eventually came to know is fascinating.

The terrestrial planets are rocky bodies. The *atmosphere* of each consists of a relatively thin layer (or no layer) of carbon dioxide or nitrogen and oxygen. The Jovian planets are much larger, but far less dense than the terrestrial planets. Most Jovian planets have an enormous atmosphere composed of hydrogen and helium. In some cases, the atmosphere may include separate layers of liquid hydrogen and metallic (but still liquid!) hydrogen. Even the rocky cores of these planets by themselves are much larger than Earth.

Although scientists now think that the interior structures of the Jovian planets are liquid or solid, these layers are composed of substances (hydrogen and helium) that we normally think of as gases. This is why the Jovian planets are more commonly referred to as the *gas giants*. (It is only

because of the incredible pressure inside the huge Jovian worlds that these substances are not gases.)

Better Views of the Planets

Even after the telescope was invented, the development of our knowledge of the planets remained rather slow. Early telescopes were very poor by today's standards. Only the most basic features of the planets were visible.

When Galileo looked at Saturn, he thought the rings around the planet were two huge moons, one on either side of the planet. It was not until the middle of the seventeenth century that astronomer and physicist Christiaan Huygens (1629–1695) could be certain that the ring he saw around Saturn was complete and that it did not touch the planet. Huygens was also the first to see a dark feature on the surface of Mars. (This triangular-shaped patch of rock-dominated land is now called Syrtis Major.)

In 1675, Jean Dominique (Giovanni Domenico) Cassini (1625–1712) was the first to see the thin, dark line that is now called the Cassini's Division. It is a gap between the two most prominent rings around Saturn.

Fortunately, the next several hundred years saw tremendous improvements in telescopes and, therefore, in the number of details detected on the surfaces or in the atmospheres of the planets. This new information enabled astronomers to begin developing theories about what con-

This *Voyager 1* photograph of Jupiter was taken from 20 million miles (33 million km) away. It shows tremendous detail in the clouds of the planet, including the giant oval of the Great Red Spot.

This Hubble Space Telescope image of Saturn
shows the different major rings and many of the dark
belts and light zones on the planet.

ditions must be like on the different worlds. Scientists also
discovered several new planets, numerous moons, and the
first asteroids (small rocky worlds that are mostly found
between the orbit of Mars and orbit of Jupiter).

Astronomers also began to understand some basics
about other types of small bodies in the solar system.
Rocky bodies smaller than asteroids are called *meteoroids*
when they are in space, *meteors* when they burn up in
Earth's atmosphere as bright "shooting stars," and *mete-*

orites on the rare occasions when they reach the ground. Icy bodies called *comets* consist of a core, or *nucleus,* and are usually several miles across. But when the comet draws close to the sun, the nucleus begins to vaporize and becomes surrounded by vast clouds of gas and dust.

At the beginning of the eighteenth century, Edmund Halley announced that he had discovered a certain comet that reappeared about every 75 years. Although he was able to correctly predict when the comet would be visible, it was not until the twentieth century that the physical nature and origins of comets were fully understood.

The most amazing discoveries in the eighteenth and nineteenth centuries were two new planets. In 1781, the German-born English astronomer Sir William Herschel (1738–1822) noticed a fuzzy dot of light that changed its position among the stars—though very slowly—from night to night and week to week. At first, Herschel supposed that he had spotted a strange, distant comet. Further observation proved that it was a planet many times larger than Earth. It was more than 1.5 billion miles (2.4 billion km) from the sun. This planet was eventually named Uranus.

The next planet was discovered in a new way—as a result of mathematical calculations. Astronomers noticed that Uranus did not always appear exactly where it should. There was something that was upsetting its orbit just a little bit. Scientists thought that an unknown planet might be tugging on Uranus ever so slightly.

In 1846, English astronomer John Couch Adams (1819–1892) and French astronomer Jean-Joseph Urbain Le Verrier (1811–1877) each calculated where such a planet would have to be. When observers looked in the sky, they spotted it. The new planet proved to be about the same size as Uranus but about a billion miles farther out. It was named Neptune.

Meanwhile, as scientists studied the complex and col-

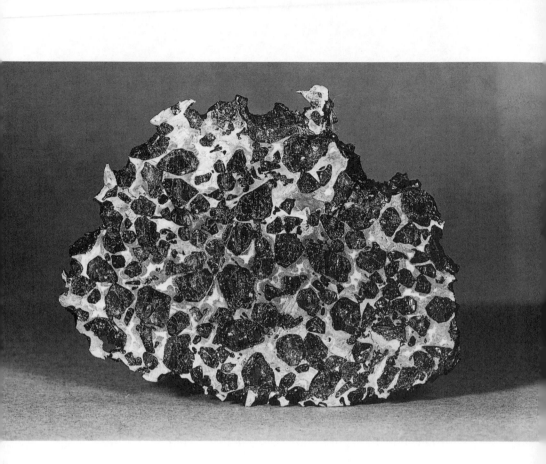

This siderite (type of stony iron meteorite) was found in Bolivia. Was it originally a piece of a comet or an asteroid?

orful cloud bands of Jupiter's atmosphere, they identified a strange enduring oval feature called the Great Red Spot among the clouds. Astronomers also proved that Saturn's rings must consist of countless pieces of ice that orbit the planet, not continuous sheets of material.

Not much more was learned about Mercury and Venus from direct observation, though. Because Mercury is so close to the sun, it was difficult to view. A nearly featureless veil of clouds hid the surface of Venus.

As the nineteenth century drew to a close, scientists were able to see many surface details of Mars at times when the planet's orbit was closest to Earth. By tracking a prominent surface feature, scientists were able to determine that the length of a day on Mars is very similar to the length of a day on Earth. They were also able to locate the poles of Mars, and found that the rotational axis of Mars had a tilt similar to that of Earth. Hence, there are Martian seasons. They observed each polar ice cap shrink when spring came to its hemisphere. At the same time, they saw dark, seemingly greenish areas in that hemisphere expand. Were scientists witnessing the spread of fresh green vegetation each Martian spring? Might there even be intelligent life on this most Earthlike of planets?

Italian astronomer Giovanni Schiaparelli (1835–1910) observed fine straight lines connecting the greenish areas on Mars and named them *canali*, an Italian word meaning "channel." The word canali does not refer to a structure made by intelligent beings as does the English word "canal." (Schiaparelli did not mean to suggest that the canali were structures built by someone to carry water.)

Nevertheless, American astronomer Percival Lowell (1855–1916) became obsessed with the idea of Martian canals. He believed that he had observed the fine straight lines on Mars on many occasions and speculated about the race of intelligent Martians who presumably made them. Twentieth-century science fiction stories, movies, and public fancy about Martians—little green men—sprang largely from Lowell's ideas. They were first used in tales written by authors H. G. Wells and Edgar Rice Burroughs.

Almost all of the lines seen by Schiaparelli, and by Lowell, were optical illusions. There are no canals on Mars, but, as we will see, there is still debate about the possibility of life on the planet.

The darker areas on this spectacular mosaic of photographs taken by a Viking Orbiter spacecraft are dominated by rock, while the lighter areas contain mostly sand. One of the Martian polar ice-caps is seen in detail.

On the Verge of the Space Age

During the first half of the twentieth century, tremendous advances were made in photography. Scientists invented a device that could quickly and easily compare photos of the same part of the sky taken at different times. Using this device allowed American astronomer Clyde Tombaugh to discover the incredibly dim and distant planet, Pluto, in 1930.

Advances were also made in *spectroscopy* (the study of the spectrum of visible light emitted or reflected by an object or area). The results can be used to determine the chemical components that an object or area contains. Spectroscopy helped determine the basic chemical make-up of planetary atmospheres.

These techniques did not, however, revolutionize the study of planets the way they did the study of stars and other objects outside our solar system. Photography of the subtlest details possible on a planet's cloud tops or surface is limited by the natural turbulence of Earth's atmosphere. The planets glow by light reflected from the sun, and the chemical identity of a planet's surface and lower atmosphere may be masked by the spectral features of its outer gases.

New techniques—listening to natural radiowave emissions from the planets, bouncing radar beams off planets, and more—were beginning to produce interesting findings. But scientists knew that the best way to learn about the planets was to send spacecraft to visit them.

The planets had gone from being points of light in the sky to subtly patterned disks in the telescope. Now it was time for them to become complex worlds, places that humans or machines could visit. It was time for scientists to learn enough about other planets to begin understanding how worlds work.

Chapter Two

Survey of the Planets

*T*hink of how exciting it must have been to live in the days when the telescope was first turned to the heavens. Every part of the sky offered a new surprise. The planets were transformed from specks of light to globes with unique characteristics.

Could there be a more thrilling time of planetary discovery than those days of Galileo and the first telescopes? Yes, we live in such a time. How could the glimpses those early telescopes gave compare in richness to the dozens upon dozens of photographs and storehouses full of other data collected in the past few decades? Thanks to the spacecraft, we have finally started to know the planets as real places, both like and unlike Earth.

Preludes to the Grand Missions

The Space Age began in 1957 when the Soviet Union launched *Sputnik*. This little spacecraft was propelled with enough speed to achieve a low orbit around Earth.

There are now thousands of these little spacecraft, called *satellites*, circling our world. Satellites in Earth orbits allow us to view the planets without interference from the thick atmosphere around and above us. These satellites also provide us with a view of our own planet from space. The photos and measurements of Earth supplied by the satellites can be directly compared to images and data collected by space probes that have been placed into orbit around other planets. It is possible to study how Earth is similar to and different from Venus or Mars when observed from a similar perspective with similar instruments.

What has captured the imaginations of people far more than even Earth-circling satellites and their fresh views of Earth are the missions to other worlds. Of course, the manned flights (first into low Earth orbit, then to the moon) of the 1960s and early 1970s gripped humanity most of all. Humans visited the moon as part of Project Apollo. The first people walked on the moon in July of 1969. For much of the 1970s and early 1980s, while the first space shuttle was being readied, there were few American manned spaceflights. These years were the first golden age for spacecraft exploration of the planets.

What came before this golden age was a tentative and incomplete reconnaissance of other worlds by *flybys*. (A flyby occurs when a spacecraft goes swiftly past a planet without achieving orbit around it.) In the early 1960s, the United States and the Soviet Union sent their first unmanned spacecraft zooming past other planets. Many of these spacecraft failed. In some cases, radio contact was lost. In other cases, their rockets misfired, causing them to miss the planets they were supposed to view by tens of millions of miles. Soviet probes did successfully reach the surface of Venus (where impact or atmospheric pressure quickly disabled them). The United States was able to

Neil Armstrong, the first human to set foot on the moon, took this classic photograph of fellow *Apollo 11* astronaut Edwin E. ("Buzz") Aldrin at Tranquility Base in July of 1969.

obtain a few close-up photos of Mars from the flybys of *Mariner 4* in 1965 and *Mariners 6* and *7* in 1969.

Then began the stunning series of successes in the 1970s and 1980s. In 1975, the Soviet Union's *Venera 9* and *10* became the first spacecraft to survive on the surface of Venus long enough to send back several photos of the dimly lit, rocky landscape. The United States' *Pioneer Venus* orbited the planet for more than a decade, sending back measurements and radar data that were used to map the surface beneath the Venusian clouds. More detailed radar mapping of Venus's topography was accomplished in the early 1990s by the United States' *Magellan* spacecraft as it orbited the planet.

Only one side of the little planet Mercury has ever been photographed close-up and that was achieved during the flybys of *Mariner 10* in 1974 and 1975.

Although the United States did not send any spacecraft to study Halley's Comet in 1986 (the Soviet Union, Japan, and the European Space Agency each did), most of the other great successes in planetary exploration during the 1970s and 1980s were achieved by the United States. The great missions to Mars, Jupiter, Saturn, and Neptune were carried out by two American space projects—Viking and Voyager.

The Viking and Voyager Missions

The Viking mission's goals were based on discoveries made by *Mariner 9*. *Mariner 9* began to orbit Mars in 1971 during a planetwide Martian dust storm that hid the entire surface of the planet. Fortunately, *Mariner 9* functioned for almost a year. When the dust settled, scientists caught their first glimpse of a world tremendously more complex, active, and beautiful than had been suspected from the earlier

Mariner flyby photos. (Those photos happened to have captured an old cratered region of the planet.)

The first objects to poke into view were the tops of volcanoes—volcanoes bigger than any mountains in the solar system.

Eventually, scientists also saw images of Valles Marineris, the Grand Canyon of Mars. Valles Marineris means "the valley of the Mariner (spacecraft)." This giant canyon is more than 3,000 miles (4,800 km) long. In fact, when it is dawn at one end of the valley, it is noon at the other end. Valles Marineris may be the result of massive stress caused by the formation of the volcanoes of what scientists call the Tharsis bulge.

Viking 1 and *2* arrived at Mars in the summer of 1976. Each spacecraft split into two portions. The *Viking Orbiters* continued to circle the planet, while the *Landers* set down safely on the surface of the planet.

The *Viking Orbiters* photographed the Martian weather (clouds, hazes, frosts) as well as the beautiful and varied terrain below. Some of these images showed features that resemble dry riverbeds and flood plains. Scientists are convinced that the riverbeds were carved out by running water. The water appears to have come up from below the planet's surface. It may have melted as the result of a volcanic eruption that warmed the area, or burst from underground springs as a result of a meteorite impact.

The *Viking Landers* photographed reddish sands and rocks (and Martian frost in winter), measured temperature and wind speed, and scooped up and analyzed Martian soil. Thanks to Viking, we know more about Mars than any other world except our own.

For Voyager, the trailblazing spacecraft were pioneers—literally, those were their names. *Pioneer 10* made its historic first pass by Jupiter in 1972. *Pioneer 11* fol-

A *Viking Lander* on Earth is shown against a painted
backdrop meant to resemble Mars. The actual landscape
of Mars proved to be considerably different.

lowed it past Jupiter in 1973 and continued on to Saturn.
When it flew past Saturn in 1979, *Pioneer 11* generated the
first images of many planetary cloud and moon surface features. These images also provided information about previously unknown moons and rings.

Unfortunately, *Pioneer 11* had to pass Saturn from an

angle that showed the night side of the rings. But the mere fact that *Pioneer 10* and *11* survived their close passes through the radiation belt of Jupiter and ring vicinity of Saturn was itself crucial information for the coming *Voyager 1* and *2*.

From 1979 to 1981, *Voyager 1* and *2* surveyed Jupiter and Saturn (and their rings and moons) far more extensively than *Pioneer 10* and *11* had done before them. Then, *Voyager 2* traveled several billion more miles away from the sun. It became the first spacecraft to pass near Uranus (1986) and Neptune (1989). These craft identified many new rings and moons and revealed their bizarre features. The information gathered by *Voyager 2* as it passed near Triton, Neptune's large moon, remains our best clue to what Pluto, the only planet still unvisited, may be like.

Before beginning our in-depth study of planetary interiors, surfaces, atmospheres, let us take a quick imaginary journey past all the planets. Along the way, you will learn about the most sensational facts and sights that have been disclosed by the spacecraft missions.

Surveying the Planets

Our tour begins where the sun looms three times larger in the sky: at the innermost planet of the solar system, Mercury.

At one time, scientists believed that Mercury was the smallest and hottest planet. Now scientists know that Pluto is the smallest and Venus is the hottest. Mercury rotates (turns around) in exactly two-thirds as much time as it takes to orbit the sun, so a given side of Mercury faces the sun most of the time.

Mercury (or at least the one side we've seen close-up) looks very much like the moon. But one major and puzzling

This image shows what *Voyager* 2 might have looked like
as it passed Uranus in January of 1986.

difference is that Mercury, unlike the moon, seems to have
a substantial magnetic field—a stronger one than that of
Mars, in fact. This suggests that Mercury may have a liquid
iron core.

Mercury also displays some surface features unlike

anything on the moon, and is marked with the Caloris Basin, the scar of an impact so large that whatever hit Mercury may have almost split the entire planet.

Next on our journey outward from the sun is Venus. There is no stranger world than Venus, and probably none that would be more difficult to live on. Even though it is twice as far from the sun as Mercury, it is the hottest planet in the solar system—about 900°F (480°C).

Venus is hotter than Mercury because it is surrounded by a thick atmosphere that contains large quantities of carbon dioxide and traps heat. The result is an enormous *greenhouse effect*. This greenhouse effect on Venus is a runaway version of Earth's much less severe, but still very worrisome, greenhouse effect some scientists believe that is causing our planet to undergo *global warming*.

The atmosphere of Venus also contains an essentially unbroken deck of yellow clouds. Soviet and American spacecraft discovered that these clouds are composed of sulfuric acid. Below these clouds are huge, possibly active, volcanoes, which may produce lightning and thunder.

Acid, heat, volcanoes, lightning—any other hazards for visitors to this hellish environment? The weight of the Venusian atmosphere is literally crushingly heavy. The surface pressure of the atmosphere on Venus is more than ninety times greater than that on Earth.

Further amazing peculiarities of Venus involve its rotation. The planet turns more slowly than it revolves around the sun. As a result, the Venusian day is longer than the Venusian year! The planet spins almost upright on its axis but backward. In other words, Venus rotates in the direction opposite to that of the other planets.

One of the most interesting topographical features of Venus is the Ishtar Terra region, which includes a huge mountain complex called Maxwell Montes.

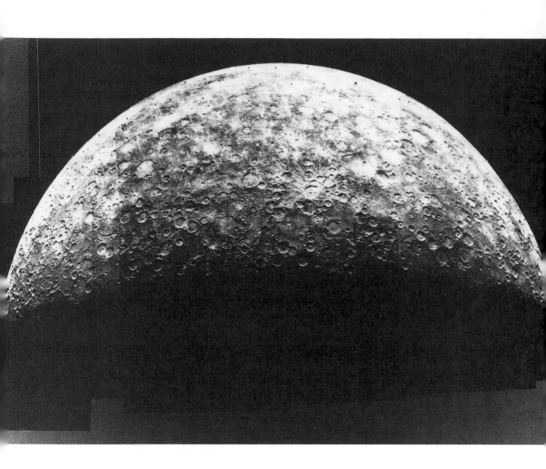

This spectacular photograph of Mercury shows that it is
even more heavily cratered than Earth's moon. It was taken
by the *Mariner 10* spacecraft from 124,000 miles
(200,000 km) away in March 1974.

Next, we cruise past our favorite world of all—Earth.
The *Galileo* spacecraft, making loops past the inner solar
system planets to pick up speed for a trip to Jupiter,
approached and passed Earth and the moon in December
1990 and 1992. From this spacecraft's unique vantage

point, it was able to take photographs that revealed some previously unrecognized features on the moon. The spacecraft also took the first movie of the entire Earth rotating.

As exciting as this was, the most important spacecraft reconnaissance of Earth has been that carried out by the satellites in Earth orbit. They have revealed vast quantities of information about the environment of our planet. These satellites can warn us about the formation of dangerous hurricanes and the buildup of environmental pollutants as well as the early effects of deforestation and desertification. (If we hope to prevent destruction from these threats, we need to know about them as soon as possible and as thoroughly as possible).

Photos of the entire Earth have done more than just inform us. They have also inspired us. They have helped many people not just know but feel in their heart that our world is precious, fragile, heartbreakingly beautiful, and irreplaceable.

Leaving aside consideration of what we've learned about that almost planetary body, the moon, we hasten onward to Mars.

You have already heard about the vast volcanoes, enormous canyon, dry riverbeds, polar ice caps, and the reddish sands of Mars. Mars has many other interesting features—the largest dune field in the solar system; the thin atmosphere that freezes and condenses on the Martian surface in the winter; the "giant's stair" terraces in the Martian "layered terrain"; the two amazingly close, irregularly shaped moons; the pink skies; the blue sunsets. These and other wonders of Mars will be considered more closely in upcoming chapters.

Next our imaginary spaceship crosses the region of the *asteroid belt*. This immense zone between the orbits of Mars and Jupiter contains countless thousands of "minor planets." Some are less than 1 mile (1.6 km) across; others are more than 600 miles (965 km) in diameter.

This photograph, which was taken by *Apollo 17* astronauts, is the most famous photo ever taken of the entire Earth. The Middle East and northern Africa are clearly visible (desert areas are frequently free of clouds).

The space between asteroids in the asteroid belt is so large that there is very little chance that a spacecraft will collide with an asteroid. Scientists planned the trajectory of the *Galileo* spacecraft so that it would pass close to two asteroids, Gaspra and Ida. The two proved quite different from each other, and both were somewhat different from what scientists expected. Ida turned out to have its own little moon (the first moon of an asteroid ever confirmed), which has been named Dactyl.

Now we have left the realm of the terrestrial planets. The first gas giant we encounter is Jupiter, the largest planet in the solar system. Its giant cloudy face is striped with dark belts and light zones. It is seething with unique phenomena with names like festoons, garlands, rifts, ovals, and spots. The most awesome of these cloud patterns is the Great Red Spot, which is three times longer than the entire Earth. Even the best Earth-based telescopes cannot show these cloud features of Jupiter with nearly as much complexity of detail as *Voyager 1* and *2* did.

But that was to be expected. Much of what the *Voyagers* found was almost completely unexpected. There was an actively volcanic moon, Io, which has literally turned itself inside out with volcanic eruptions in the course of its lifetime. There were *auroras*, superlightning, and electroglow. There were even dim, but dramatic, rings around Jupiter.

Something else that wasn't expected occurred at Jupiter in July 1994. The pieces of a comet, Shoemaker-Levy 9, showered down on the atmosphere of the planet. The impacts produced a number of vast dark spots above the cloud tops of Jupiter. These remained visible for about 6 months after the impact. The exact nature of the spots has yet to be determined.

After traversing the gap between the largest planet and the second-largest, we reach Saturn. Its rings and moons are far from disappointing. It has seven major rings (including a seemingly braided one) made up of about a thousand smaller "ringlets"—some lopsided, some kinked, some being held in place by *shepherd satellites*. We also see dark mysterious patterns that look like spokes rotating with the rings.

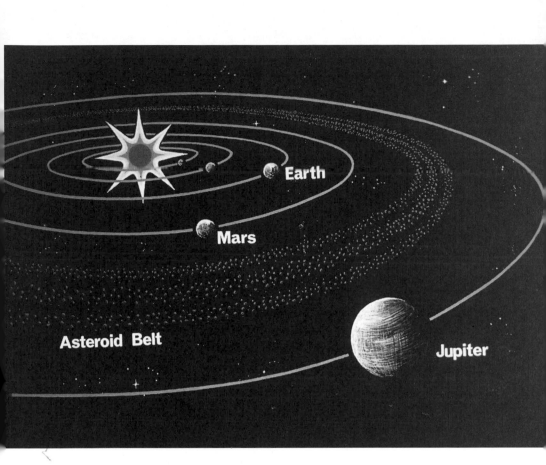

This diagram shows the approximate location of the
asteroid belt. There are a number of individual belts
(three are suggested here).

The moons come in so many arrangements and such
battered forms as to stagger the imagination. Two Saturnian
moons appear to trade places with each other. They may be
the halves of a larger moon that broke apart. Other moons
follow each other around in the same orbit. Still others may

43

have broken into pieces and then reformed. One moon rotates completely chaotically—there is no pattern to the changes in length of day and the cardinal directions on this moon. The atmosphere of another moon is denser than Earth's. One moon is thirteen times brighter on one side than it is on the other. What a challenge it is to make sense of the complex but majestic oddities of the great Saturnian rings and moons!

Our imaginary ship next comes to a planet that only *Voyager 2* has encountered—Uranus. Due to a high-altitude haze and the coldness that comes with great distance from the sun, the cloud tops of this gas giant are virtually featureless. In 1993, a telescope on Earth successfully photographed a large spot in the clouds of Uranus. Perhaps its upper atmosphere is not always as placid and uneventful as it happened to be when *Voyager 2* passed in January 1986. The Hubble Space Telescope has revealed additional cloud features of Uranus.

Uranus has sparse, dark, barely visible rings that roll around the orbit of Uranus like a wheel because the planet rotates *on its side*. In other words, its rotational axis is close to 90° different from its orbital path. Scientists knew about the strange orientation of the Uranian axis long before *Voyager 2* visited or the first rings of the planet were discovered (the rings of Uranus were discovered when they passed in front of a star in 1977).

How did scientists know about the axis of Uranus? They knew about it because when moons are relatively close to a much more massive planet they are always found to orbit almost right over the equator of the planet. The five moons of Uranus that have been known for decades are all circling the planet at almost right angles to the orbit.

Photos taken by *Voyager* have allowed scientists to identify more rings and moons (ten more) around Uranus.

Here is an artist's conception of what Pluto may look like from its moon Charon. No spacecraft has yet visited these worlds.

One moon, named Miranda, has a surface that resembles a patchwork quilt. It appears to have fallen back together after being shattered. On the surface of Miranda are tall cliffs—they may be 12 miles (19 km) high! They are the tallest cliffs yet discovered in the solar system.

Data from Voyager also revealed that the magnetic poles of Uranus are way out of line with its rotational axis and its orbital path.

Scientists were startled by what *Voyager 2* discovered at Neptune. Even though it is almost a billion miles farther from the sun than Uranus, it has "weather." Cameras on *Voyager 2* revealed a Great Dark Spot, a number of clouds, and other features in its atmosphere. The heat source for this weather must be the planet's central regions, which are hot from being compressed by all the layers of Neptune above it. Neptune's use of that heat must be extremely efficient.

Like Jupiter, Saturn, and Uranus, Neptune too has rings. The Neptunian rings are inconspicuous, almost fragmentary. Voyager also allowed scientists to identify many more moons orbiting Neptune. One of Neptune's moons, called Triton, is the only large one in the solar system to travel retrograde (backward) in its orbit. Triton's surface has several types of radically different terrain. One part of Triton's surface looks much like the outside of a cantaloupe. The planet may also have volcanoes that gush liquid nitrogen on its surface.

Our final stop is at a world that, in 1999, will again become the most distant planet in our solar system. Tiny Pluto has not yet been visited by a spacecraft, so scientists can only speculate about it on the basis of information obtained during such special events as its rare eclipses with its large moon, Charon. Pluto and Charon are amazingly close to each other and rotate so that one face of the planet always faces a particular face of the moon. Pluto's rotation is backward, and slow. (It takes more than six *Earth days* for it to turn around once.) Pluto also takes more than 248 Earth years to circle the sun once. What we know about Pluto's size, chemistry, and temperature suggests it may be somewhat like Triton. But when one of our spacecraft is finally sent to Pluto, we may find that we're in for more planetary surprises.

Chapter Three

Planetary Interiors and Magnetospheres

*N*ow that we have surveyed the growth of knowledge about the planets and some of the outstanding facts and features of the worlds, it is time to begin a more in-depth study of the planets. In this chapter, you examine planetary interiors and the magnetic fields they create.

The Cores and Interiors of Planets

Scientists know far less about the interiors of planets than they know about their surfaces and atmospheres. Even here on Earth, very little is known about the rocks just a few miles beneath our feet. Most of this rock is untouched and unseen. It is inaccessible to almost every kind of measuring instrument scientists have developed. Next to nothing is known about the center of our planet, which is about 4,000 miles (6,400 km) below us. Even less is known about the interiors of other planets.

Before scientists can begin to make predictions about the interiors of other planets, they must know the mass and size of the planets, their distances from the sun, and the relative amounts of the chemicals that make up the planets. This last requirement is the difficult one.

Ideally, scientists could use the best theories of solar system formation to estimate how much of various elements and compounds may have existed at, say, Jupiter's distance from the sun when Jupiter formed 4.5 billion years ago. Unfortunately, there are still major uncertainties about the formation of the solar system.

Even if scientists could determine the chemical composition of a planet, it would be difficult to determine how these chemical substances would behave under the incredibly great pressures and temperatures deep within planets. Even small differences in these variables can vastly change the behavior of a substance. (Consider, for example, that a difference of 1°F can mean the difference between an inch of rain and a foot of snow.)

The region below Earth's crust (outermost layer) is called the *mantle*. Scientists believe that the pressure in the mantle is great enough to make solid rock flow! Direct support for this contention comes from *seismographs*, which detect pressure waves (usually from earthquakes) as they travel through different sections of Earth. Seismographs have been left on both the moon and Mars to record interior pressure fluctuations. Another way to determine how matter is concentrated in different parts of a planet is to study the gravitational effect that different regions of a world have on the path of an orbiting spacecraft.

The gas giants have much larger atmospheres than the terrestrial planets. As a result, the inner regions of these planets are under more pressure than the inner regions of terrestrial planets. Because tremendously high pressure produces higher temperatures, it is reasonable to suppose that temperatures within the gas giants are also greater than temperatures within the terrestrial planets. Our spacecraft have helped verify this theory.

The *Voyager*s found much more heat coming from the interior of Jupiter than the planet receives from the sun. If Jupiter were much more massive, the planet's hydrogen would undergo a *thermonuclear reaction*.

In other words, Jupiter would become a sun, a star. If it were perhaps ten times more massive, it would have become self-luminous and we would be living in a *double star system*. Double star systems are very common. At least half of all stars may be members of double star systems.

Interior Cause of Planetary Magnetic Fields

A key question about the interiors of terrestrial planets is whether or not they have a differentiated core (a central region that is composed of different materials than the layers above). While there is no way for scientists to know all of the materials within the cores of the planets, they can try to determine whether a planet's core is differentiated using some logical considerations.

For instance, according to the rules of geometry, a small world has more surface area relative to its mass than a large world does. As a result, the interior of a small world will cool more rapidly than the interior of a large one. If a planet cools quickly, the iron in its core will not have enough time to settle into a distinct central core.

Can scientists measure anything that would indicate whether a planet has a differentiated iron core? Yes, scientists can measure magnetic fields. Strong planetary magnetic fields are believed to be generated by the motion of iron in a planet's core. Earth has the strongest magnetic field of the terrestrial planets. Although Mercury possesses a far weaker field, it is much stronger than scientists expected (and that remains a mystery). Mars also has a weak magnetic field.

Although Venus possesses a significant field, it is generated by the impact of charged particles from the sun with the gases of the planet's ionosphere. Does this mean that there is no iron core in Venus? No, not necessarily. Because Venus rotates hundreds of times more slowly than Earth, any motion in the core would be extremely sluggish and, therefore, generate a very weak field.

The gas giants all rotate much faster than Earth and their magnetic fields range from fairly strong to immensely powerful. Interestingly, it is the higher interior layers, not the cores, of these planets that produce the magnetic fields. These fields are generated in layers composed of liquid metallic hydrogen.

Scientists have been able to detect evidence of particles from the solar wind trapped in Jupiter's very strong magnetic field. (These particles interact with atoms of sodium and other materials ejected from Io, a Jovian moon with volcanic activity.) The trapped particles form belts of radiation around the planet. (The radiation is so strong that astronauts would need special shielding to be safe.)

Like Jupiter, Earth is surrounded by belts of radiation. These *Van Allen Belts* of radiation, which are far less intense than those surrounding Jupiter, are produced by the interaction of particles from the sun with Earth's magnetic field. Two of these belts were discovered early in the history of the Space Age, and a third belt was identified more recently.

Saturn traps far less radiation in belts because the mighty rings interfere with the process.

Uranus has a magnetic field tilted strangely far off from both its rotational axis (which, remember, is almost in the plane of the planet's orbit) and the direction perpendicular

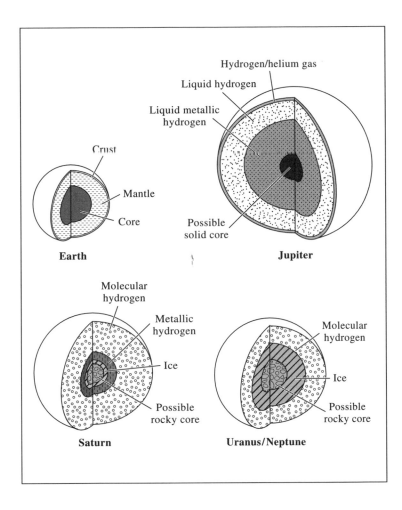

Scientists believe that the core of Jupiter, the largest
plant in the solar system, has a mass 10 to 20 times
greater than that of Earth. The inner rocky core of Saturn
may have a mass 20 times greater than that of Earth.
Because Uranus and Neptune have the same mass
and bulk composition, scientists believe that their
interiors are very similar. Their rocky cores may have
masses about 10 times greater than that of Earth.

to its orbital plane. Surely the odd tilt of the magnetic field has something to do with Uranus's rotating-on-its-side posture.

Strangely enough, *Voyager 2* found that Neptune (which rotates at only a slight tilt with respect to its rotational axis) has almost exactly as extreme a tilt to its magnetic field as Uranus. In addition, its magnetic axis is offset a large distance from the planet's center. The magnetic field of Neptune is surprisingly weak—much weaker than Earth's.

The diagrams above show the interior structures of the gas giants, as projected by some scientists. Remember that these are speculative. Note the similarities between the interior structures of Uranus and Neptune, and between Jupiter and Saturn. Saturn is by far the least dense of the planets. Its average density is much less than that of water.

Magnetospheres

The magnetic fields of planets and comets interact with the plasma of charged subatomic particles released by the sun. This outflow of particles—mostly electrons and protons— is called the *solar wind*. If a planetary magnetic field is strong enough to deflect the solar wind, it forms a protective cavity around the planet called the *magnetosphere* (the region in which the plasma conditions of the planet's magnetic field are maintained). The solar wind closes in on and mixes with the magnetosphere plasma in a long, narrow structure beyond the planet on the side of the planet facing away from the sun. (This phenomenon is similar to the tail of a comet, except that the gas is not plentiful enough or energized enough to glow visibly.) In the case of Jupiter, this "magnetic tail" extends all the way out beyond the orbit of Saturn, so that Saturn can actually pass through it!

This shot of the aurora australis was taken
by the space shuttle.

Even though we cannot see Earth's magnetic tails, or
those of other planets, we can sometimes see a related phenomenon. I am referring to the Northern Lights and the
Southern Lights, which are actually visible in both far
northern and far southern regions of Earth. These dancing
patterns of colored light in our skies are the result of a spe-

cial interaction between Earth's magnetic field and the solar wind.

Scientists call these lights auroras. Scientists still have much to learn about auroras, but they have identified several solar events that can produce them. One such event is a *solar flare* (an outburst of the sun that sends large quantities of protons and electrons our way on the solar wind). Earth's magnetic field somehow magnifies the energy of these particles and they are channeled by Earth's lines of magnetic force toward oval regions around Earth's magnetic poles. In those regions, the particles collide with gases in our planet's upper atmosphere. These gases (mostly oxygen and nitrogen), which are located about 50 to 500 miles (80 to 800 km) above Earth's surface, behave much like the gas in a fluorescent light or neon light tube. Just as the electric current we turn on provides the energy required to operate a fluorescent or neon light, the solar particles and Earth's magnetic field provide an aurora's energy.

You would expect that the gas giants, with strong magnetic fields and upper atmospheric gases that can be energized, would also have auroral displays. Indeed, the *Voyager*s have shown that Jupiter has extremely powerful auroras. Uranus too shows prominent auroras, apparently stronger than Saturn's.

Chapter Four

Planetary Surfaces

$\mathcal{W}$e know a great deal about the surfaces of the terrestrial planets and almost nothing about the gas giants. This is because we can see the surfaces of all of the terrestrial planets except Venus. And as you learned in Chapter 2, the secrets of Venus's topography have been revealed to scientists by radar-imaging techniques.

Erosion

Let's begin our comparison of planetary surfaces with a look at a surface-altering process that Mercury and the moon don't have, but Mars and Venus clearly do: erosion.

Erosion can be produced by wind or water. The thin atmosphere of Mars has not been able to erode away its old impact craters the way that Earth's and Venus's atmospheres have. But, as we'll see later in this book, the atmosphere does transport large quantities of dust around Mars. This is accomplished by strong winds and by the condensing and

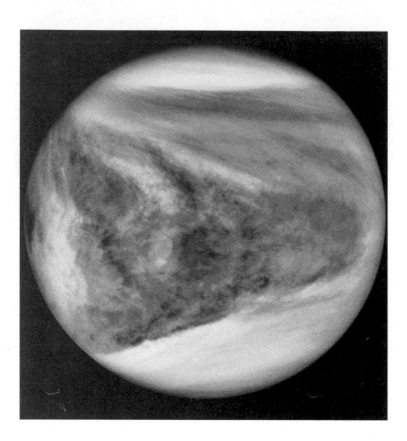

This photograph of Venus was taken by the *Pioneer* Orbiter. The planet's sulfuric acid clouds are clearly visible.

freezing of much of the Martian atmosphere in the hemisphere experiencing winter.

Both Mars and Venus show certain indications of once having had rivers, even oceans of water. Those of Mars have unquestionably left their erosional mark.

The famous reddish dust of Mars gives the planet a slight ruddiness detectable, even with the naked eye, from

Earth. The areas of Mars that look like dark greenish markings in telescopes are regions in which there is more bare rock and less dust. The greenish hue is an illusion, a color the eye produces in response to the predominant reddish coloration of the surrounding globe. The reddish hue of the dust, however, is quite real. It is caused by iron compounds in the dust. The dust of Venus, when seen in a neutral light, has a more grayish color.

Perhaps the most provocative landforms on Mars are the dry riverbeds. There can be no doubt, considering their shapes and sources, that these various-sized channels were carved out by running water. Because evidence has shown that water flowed on the Martian surface only briefly, scientists believe that most of the channels were formed by the flow of water when subsurface ice was melted by meteorite impacts or when volcanoes warmed or shook an area, causing water to burst from underground springs.

Plate Tectonics and Volcanoes

A key distinction between Earth's surface and those of neighboring worlds is that it has been formed—and continues to be formed—by *plate tectonics*. Most of Earth's topography can be explained by the interactions between the enormous slowly moving "plates" of rock on which the surface rests. When these plates collide, new mountain ranges may push up through Earth's surface. When the plates pull away from each other, new material may form new regions of seafloor.

Only Earth seems to have horizontal plate motions. Mercury and the moon have been geologically dead for a long time. Some of Mercury's unusual surface features seem to be cracks that formed when the planet cooled and shrank. Those cracks would not appear as they do if the surface of Mercury were not one single plate.

Mars and Venus must have been—and may still be—somewhat more geologically active than Mercury and the moon. Both Mars and Venus possess volcanoes that may still be active. Does this mean there is horizontal plate movement on Mars and Venus?

The answer is, apparently not. Some of the volcanoes and other mountains of Venus and Mars are quite spectacular. Venus, for instance, offers the Ishtar Terra region, a lofty upland about the size of Australia. It includes Maxwell Montes, a huge mountain complex that is taller than Earth's Mt. Everest.

I have already mentioned the giant volcanoes of Mars and its mighty canyon system Valles Marineris. The biggest mountain, Olympus Mons, may tower as high as 17 miles (31 km) above surrounding terrain and spread out with a very gentle slope to encompass an area about as large as the state of Missouri. Olympus Mons and its three fellow giant volcanoes (a trio standing in an almost perfect line) are located on a truly enormous raised landmass called Tharsis. The Tharsis bulge is so tall and large that scientists believe its formation must have radically changed the axis tilt of the entire planet!

The Valles Marineris is so long (more than 3,000 miles, or 4,800 km) that when one end is experiencing noon the

The *Magellan* spacecraft photographed this section of Venus's surface in 1990. At the top right is Lakshmi Planum, a smooth plain. Below the plain is Danu Montes, which forms the southern boundary of Ishtar Terra, the northern hemisphere continent.

other is experiencing dawn. The result is a huge temperature difference, which must cause strong winds to blow down the canyon. Valles Marineris leads away from Tharsis and must be a result of the stress caused by the birth and growth of Tharsis.

But what caused Tharsis itself? Is the crust under this region weak, thus permitting upwelling and outflow of lava? Or was Tharsis the result of an unprecedentedly cataclysmic disruption inside the depths of Mars?

Although scientists do not know the answers to these questions, they do know that the type of geological activity of Venus and Mars is very different from geological activity on Earth. To sum it up succinctly, whatever plate movement there has been—and may still be—within the surfaces of Mars and perhaps Venus has been vertical, not horizontal.

A superb example of this distinction is provided by comparison of Mars's mighty Tharsis volcanoes and Earth's Hawaiian volcanoes. The two largest examples of each are Mars's Olympus Mons and Hawaii's Mauna Loa. The latter is actually Earth's biggest mountain, if measured from the seafloor up. But it is many times smaller than Olympus Mons.

Both volcanoes are of the same type: they are *shield volcanoes* (volcanoes with comparatively nonexplosive eruptions of fairly thin runny lava, which is produced in immense quantities and slowly accumulates on their sides, making for gentle slopes).

This spectacular mosaic of *Viking Orbiter* photos shows the mighty Valles Marineris canyon system (cutting horizontally across the lower middle of the image). Three of the big Tharsis volcanoes are visible at the far left of the image.

So why are Olympus Mons and the other Tharsis volcanoes so much larger than Mauna Loa and the other Hawaiian volcanoes? They are larger because Earth's tectonic plates move onward past the deep source of the lava. As a result, that source gives rise to one volcano after another—one Hawaiian Island after another. Each volcano moves off the upwelling vent before it can build up to anything like Olympus Mons's size.

The Tharsis bulge of Mars is apparently not on a horizontally moving plate. Consequently, as long as the deep magma sources beneath Olympus Mons and the other Tharsis volcanoes stay active, these Martian volcanoes will keep spewing out lava, which will harden on their sides to make them larger and larger. This has presumably been happening for hundreds of millions of years.

Impacts and Cratered Terrain

One of the most important forces shaping the surface of planets is meteorite and asteroid impacts.

Most researchers believe that about 65 million years ago an impact (or, rather its aftereffects) killed off the dinosaurs. Asteroid (or comet) collisions of this magnitude are very rare.

In the earliest days of the solar system (4 to 4.5 billion years ago), however, meteorite, asteroid, and comet bombardments were more common. During this time, all of the terrestrial planets were struck and severely cratered.

Today, these wounds are visible only on the moon and Mercury. These small worlds had too little gravity to hold on to their atmospheres for very long and too little mass to remain geologically active. Because the moon and Mercury have no atmosphere, they have no protection from meteoroids. (Earth's atmosphere acts as a protective shield.

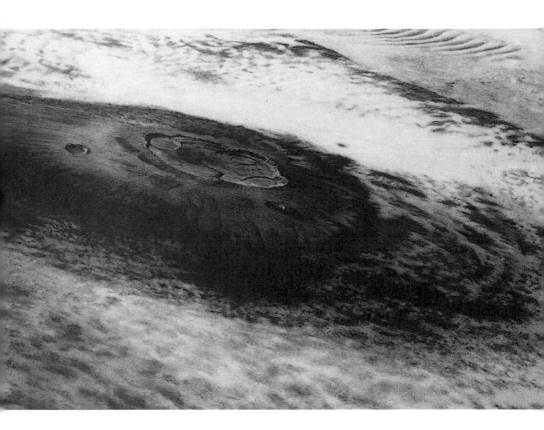

This view of Olympus Mons was taken by the *Viking Orbiter.*

Most of the meteoroids that enter our planet's atmosphere burn up as meteors before they reach the surface.)

No atmosphere also means no weather. There is no wind or water to erode away the craters left by meteorites. These worlds also have no volcanic activity—no lava spilling or ground upheavals to cover the craters. When you look at the cratered terrains of the Moon and Mercury, you are seeing truly ancient land, land not greatly changed from the way it was when the solar system was young.

The other terrestrial planets are not without their craters, of course. On Venus, the ancient surface has been altered by some geologic activity and weather produced within its heavy atmosphere. One half of Mars's surface consists of ancient cratered terrain. The other half has been churned by the planet's internal activity.

Earth has the youngest and freshest surface of all. Only about 15 percent of Earth's surface is ancient terrain (notably much of the northern part of North America). Most of Earth's original surface has been pushed under a tectonic plate during a plate collision. Some parts of Earth's surface have also been thrust up by plate collisions to form mountain ranges. Other parts of the surface (the mid-ocean ridges) have been pushed up as part of a process called ocean-floor spreading.

The Importance of Earth's Oceans

The mention of mid-oceanic ridges and ocean-floor spreading raises the topic of oceans and water on the planets. Not all oceans are made of water—some of the worlds of the outer solar system may have chilly seas of liquid ammonia. Similarly, a planet may have large quantities of water, but no oceans, or lakes, or rivers. Scientists believe that there are large quantities of water in Jupiter's atmosphere.

Earth is the only planet with large quantities of liquid water covering its surface. Water covers about 71 percent of Earth's surface, while land covers just 29 percent. There is thirteen times more water below sea level than land above sea level. In fact, scientists sometimes call Earth "the Water Planet."

It's important to remember that most of the world's water is undrinkable. Ninety-seven percent of the world's water is seawater. In the past few decades, humans have rendered much of the remaining 3 percent unfit to drink. No one has yet figured out a way to make running desalinization plants or towing icebergs economically feasible for most of the world's population—so we had better take care.

Earth has four oceans—the Pacific, Atlantic, Indian, and Arctic—and thirty-two seas. The Pacific is the largest ocean. It covers about one-third of Earth's surface—more area than all of Earth's land combined. Orbiting astronauts have been struck by how much of the Earth's surface is covered by water—by how even at about 18,000 mph (29,000 km/hr.) it takes a significant amount of time to cross the Pacific. According to one estimate, the Pacific Ocean contains about 3.5 sextillion (3,500,000,000,000,000,000,000) gallons (13.3 sextillion liters) of water.

Close to 11 percent of Earth's land is covered by ice—some of it miles thick. Greenhouse warming may melt this ice and cause thermal expansion of the oceans. If this happens, even more of Earth's surface will be covered with water by the middle of the next century.

Water covers more than 80 percent of Earth's southern hemisphere, but only about 57 percent of the northern hemisphere. Look at a globe with Normandy, France at the center of your view. Now, turn the globe until New Zealand is at the center. What do you notice?

Normandy is close to the land pole, while New Zealand is close to Earth's water pole. Even though only 29 percent of Earth's surface is covered by land, most of this land is concentrated in one area of the globe. The half of Earth surrounding the water pole is little more than a giant ocean with a few very large islands (like Australia and Antarctica) in it.

Life arose in the oceans. All land-dwelling creatures need water to survive. The human body is more than 75 percent water, and our blood is about as salty as ocean water. We are like worlds ourselves—each carrying his or her precious interior sea.

Water on Venus and Mars

The other terrestrial planets lack areas of free surface water. Mars has features (dry riverbeds, vast dry floodplains), which suggest that at one time there was water on its surface. There also may have been a small, shallow Martian ocean. Some scientists believe that all these bodies of water were very temporary phenomena, that Mars lost its atmosphere early. When a planet loses its atmosphere, the reduced air pressure allows water to evaporate more easily. Then, like other gases, the water vapor is slowly lost to space.

Mars does possess a water supply, perhaps even a fairly large one. Am I referring to the Martian polar ice caps? No. While it's true that the Martian ice caps do contain some water, the real hope for a supply of water on Mars comes from the ground. Scientists believe that a large quantity of water is frozen in the soil.

What is the evidence for this? If you look at meteorite craters, you will notice that they are surrounded by undulating ridges. These ridges may remind you of what happens when a rock is dropped into a puddle of mud. When a meteorite strikes a surface, a great deal of heat is released. It is possible that the undulating ridges form when a meteorite strikes soil containing frozen water, the water thaws, and a mudflow occurs. Just how much water, how near the surface, is frozen in Mars remains to be discovered. The answer could certainly be important to our hopes of colonizing the planet.

Venus may have also had an ocean in its early days—perhaps a fairly deep planetwide one. Before scientists can determine how much water was once on Venus, they must develop a better way to measure a substance called *deuterium*.

Other Major Influences in the Making of Planetary Surfaces

There is so much to say about the surfaces of the terrestrial planets that it is impossible to discuss most of the particulars. But we can summarize the major influences on the development of the planets' surfaces.

First, the size of the planet matters. This is true not only because the size (and mass) may determine whether a planet's atmosphere will survive and erosional processes will occur. It is also true because smaller planets cool more efficiently than large ones. There's little doubt that the relatively quick cooling of Mercury is responsible for some of its geologic features. These planetary cracks formed in the same way as wrinkles in a cooling baked apple.

A second major influence on a planetary surface is the chemical makeup of the planet. This varies with distance from the sun because temperature and pressure decrease as one moves outward from the center of the cloud of gas and dust in which scientists believe the solar system formed.

A third critical influence on planetary surfaces is sources of energy. Most of the energy in the solar system comes from the sun. Some of the energy available to a planet may come from its interior (natural radioactive materials), tidal interactions with other bodies in space, or meteorite and comet impacts. Impacts as a source of energy for surface changes are a real "wild card" because very large impacts are infrequent and unpredictable.

Pluto

Scientists know very little about the surface of Pluto because no spacecraft has passed near the planet. The best they can do is make guesses on the basis of evidence collected during Earth-based studies.

During the 1980s, scientists observed rare mutual eclipses of Pluto and Charon (its moon). They learned that the two bodies are quite different in composition. Pluto contains a much higher percentage of rock to ice than Charon does. Brightness variations of Pluto and spectroscopic studies of it suggest that the planet is partly covered with methane ice. This ice becomes a thin atmosphere when the planet is close to the sun.

Pluto is about the same size as Triton (a moon of Neptune). The two worlds are presently about the same distance from the sun, and are displaying some similar behaviors. Some scientists used to believe that Pluto could have been a moon of Neptune, and that a third large body knocked Pluto out of its orbit. The same large body may have somehow knocked Triton into its strange retrograde orbit.

But there are plenty of reasons to doubt this idea. In fact, since *Voyager 2*'s visit to Neptune and Triton, scientists have speculated that Triton is itself a captured moon. Objects like Triton and Pluto might have been common once, and their smaller relatives (mostly comets) may still exist not much farther out from the sun.

In the early 1990s a number of bodies of this sort were identified. Some are in circular orbits even larger than Pluto's. (As you'll learn in Chapter 7, these objects may be the comets.)

Life as a Changer of Planetary Surfaces

When all of the planets are considered, volcanic activity and meteorite collisions have influenced planetary surfaces more than anything else. On Earth, however, the presence of life has also transformed Earth's surface and atmosphere.

These changes began about 400 million years ago, as plants began to invade the land. Over millions of years, these plants released large quantities of oxygen into the atmosphere. It is this oxygen that made animal life possible.

A surprising fact about life on Earth—including that active and meddlesome species called humans—is that until recently, it had made no change to Earth's surface that would signify its presence to viewers on another planet. Just as scientists were once unsure about whether the greenish-gray areas on Mars were vegetation, Martians—if they existed—would be unsure about the source of green or dark areas (great forests) on Earth. Civilization's greatest cities and other enormous land use projects have not yet produced marks that can be readily seen from other planets.

If Martians wanted direct proof of intelligent life on Earth, they would have to view our planet's night side. What would they see in their telescopes? They would be able to spot the glow of light given off by Earth's greatest cities.

This city lighting display is not one we should be proud of, however. The glow is caused by *light pollution* (excess or misdirected outdoor lighting) flying off wastefully into space. It costs the citizens of Earth billions of dollars every year. It is these same bright lights that prevent most nighttime skygazers from seeing many of the amazing features of the starry heavens.

If you're interested in learning more about light pollution and how you can do your part to fight it, write to:

The International Dark-sky Association
3545 N. Stewart Ave.
Tucson, AZ 85716

Of course, just because there is no other indication of human presence to an observer in space doesn't mean that our activities aren't having an impact on the planet. Some of the effects of human actions—polluted rivers, abandoned strip mines, nuclear waste dumps—are causing great damage. Environmentalists warn us that even the most seemingly beneficial human actions may produce unfortunate results that could not have been foreseen.

We have come to a time in history when one form of life, by its conscious yet sometimes thoughtless actions, can unleash forces that can transform the entire planet. Many of the most detrimental changes are not directly visible. You cannot see the gases destroying our *ozone layer*, but many of us may see and feel the results. The dangers we are unleashing on our world and ourselves give the study of planetology a new sense of urgency.

Chapter Five

Planetary Atmospheres

*T*he solid crust of a planet's surface is called the *litho-sphere*, and Earth's vast expanses of water form its *hydro-sphere*. The gaseous part of a planet is called its atmosphere.

In the cases of the terrestrial planets, the atmospheres are tiny and seemingly insubstantial compared to the solid bulk of the planets themselves. If you travel 5 miles (8 km) above sea level on Earth, most of the atmosphere will be below you. If you travel another 50 to 100 miles (80 to 160 km) up, you will be in space. If you look at a map, you will see that space may be closer to you than the capital of your home state.

This rather flimsy atmosphere of ours is absolutely essential to almost all life on Earth. It does more than just provide the oxygen animals need to power their bodies. We are all now aware (or should be!) that the ozone layer in our atmosphere protects us from the sun's ultraviolet radiation. If you are ready to plunge into the study of our atmosphere and those of the other worlds in our solar system, take a deep—and I hope delicious—breath and read on!

Gas Giant versus Terrestrial Planet Atmospheres

The atmospheres of the gas giant planets are tremendously greater than those of the terrestrial planets. This is true both in absolute terms (Saturn's atmosphere is hundreds of times deeper than Earth's) and in terms of the percentage of the planet that is atmosphere (Earth's atmosphere is much thinner compared to its solid bulk than an orange peel is to an orange). The differences between gas giant atmospheres and terrestrial atmospheres are much more profound than differences in size, however.

The atmospheres of the gas giants have retained much of the gas from the formation of the solar system, while those of the terrestrial planets have not. The atmospheres of the Jovian worlds are predominantly hydrogen—either in its free state or in compounds like ammonia (NH_3) and methane (CH_4). Hydrogen, which is the element with the simplest atomic structure, is by far the most common element in the sun and throughout the universe.

When the solar system formed, all of the planets (terrestrial and gas giants) were enshrouded in hydrogen. Today, Mercury has no atmosphere, Earth's atmosphere is composed primarily of nitrogen and oxygen, and the atmospheres of Venus and Mars are composed primarily of carbon dioxide. (Actually, at any given time, there may be tiny traces of outgassing vapors detectable around Mercury—and the moon—but the amount is negligible.)

Why don't the terrestrial planets have large amounts of hydrogen in their atmospheres today? The terrestrial planets are much smaller than the gas giants. Smaller size means less gravitational pull. Because hydrogen is the lightest, simplest element, it was able to escape from the atmospheres of the planets with less gravity.

The terrestrial planets are also warmer than the gas giants. When the atoms in hydrogen, or any other substance, are warmer, they move more quickly. Faster-moving atoms can fly off into space more easily than colder, slower-moving atoms.

Earth, Venus, and Mars were able to keep atmospheres containing slightly heavier elements (nitrogen, oxygen, carbon dioxide). Mercury lost all of the gases in its atmosphere because it is very small and very hot. (Likewise, it was not just the massive concentrations of matter which formed beyond the asteroid belt that helped retain hydrogen in the atmospheres of the gas giants; it was also the lower temperatures out there.)

Gas Giant Atmospheres

The difference between a gas giant atmosphere and a terrestrial planet atmosphere is certainly obvious. But, in our study of atmospheres, we can differentiate further and distinguish the atmospheres of Uranus and Neptune as being quite different from those of Jupiter and Saturn.

The atmospheres of all four gas giants are composed primarily of hydrogen and helium. While the atmospheres of Jupiter and Saturn also contain a great deal of ammonia, those of Neptune and Uranus contain little ammonia. Instead they contain large quantities of methane. You can see this difference by looking at the planets through a telescope. While the predominant color of Jupiter and Saturn is yellow, Uranus and Neptune are blue or blue-green. These planets look bluish because methane in their atmospheres filters out red wavelengths of sunlight.

Our finest overall view of Neptune may be this mosaic from
Voyager 2's flyby in 1989. The Great Dark Spot is plainly
visible, as are white clouds and many other features.

Apart from this difference, there are other reasons
that scientists often break the gas giants into two categories. Uranus and Neptune are much less massive, much
more dense, and much farther from the sun than Jupiter
and Saturn.

Cloud-top temperature is –260°F (–162°C) for Jupiter, –290°F (–178°C) for Saturn, and –357°F (–216°C) for both Uranus and Neptune. The fact that the much more distant Neptune has the same cloud-top temperature as Uranus is somewhat puzzling.

The Atmosphere of Venus

Even though Venus is only slightly smaller than Earth, and the two come closer together in space than any other planets do, Venus is astonishingly different from our world. As you learned in Chapter 2, the atmosphere of Venus exerts about ninety times more pressure on that planet's surface than Earth's atmosphere exerts on our own planet. The Venusian atmosphere is so heavy that standing on its surface would be like standing at the bottom of the ocean under half a mile of water!

The atmosphere of Venus is composed almost entirely of carbon dioxide. The greenhouse effect caused by this substance heats the planet up to about 900°F (480°C)—and not just on the day side. Apparently, the planet's atmosphere and permanent cloud cover insulate so well that the temperature does not decrease at night. The thick air and the layer of cloud high in the atmosphere block out most of the sun's rays. A typical day on Venus is no brighter than a very cloudy day on Earth.

As we noted earlier, the cloud-deck of Venus is composed of sulfuric acid droplets. A much less dense layer of sulfuric acid droplets is present in Earth's atmosphere for a few years after a major volcanic eruption. Such eruptions include those of El Chichon volcano in 1982 and Mt. Pinatubo in 1991.

Air probably moves very slowly near the surface of Venus, but in the upper atmosphere winds may move at

This *Mariner 10* shot of Venus in ultraviolet light shows details in the ever present clouds, which block most light from getting to the planet's surface.

very great speeds. In fact, the clouds of Venus seem to travel around the entire planet in about 4 days, a stunning contrast to the creepingly slow pace of the surface, which takes about 8 months to complete one rotation.

If the volcanoes of Venus are still occasionally erupting, their clouds may generate enough electric charges to produce lightning. Observers have occasionally noticed an auroralike glow on the night side of Venus. Scientists do not know what causes this "Ashen Light." It may be produced when particles from the sun strike the upper atmosphere, or it could it be some kind of optical illusion.

The Atmosphere of Earth

Earth's atmosphere is about 78 percent nitrogen and 21 percent oxygen (the remaining 1 percent is other gases). No other planet's atmosphere has such a high percentage of oxygen. A little less oxygen in our atmosphere would endanger many species, while a little more would make fires far more frequent and dangerous.

It is difficult to talk about the atmosphere of Earth without talking about its partner: the hydrosphere. Water vapor in the atmosphere forms clouds and produces rain and other types of precipitation. Most of this water eventually ends up in Earth's lakes, rivers, and oceans. The water evaporates into the air, and the whole cycle begins again.

This evaporative cycle is the key to the weather and climate of Earth. Weather is the short-term atmospheric condition for a place; climate is the long-term one. Both are products of atmosphere and hydrosphere, of air and water.

The oceans of the world respond to changes in temperature far more slowly than the air. As a result, they eliminate the extremes of climate and weather. You may have noticed that the weather at the seashore is usually less hot in the summer and less cold in the winter, or that the ocean temperature lags behind the air temperature. (The ocean is cooler than the air as summer starts and warmer than the air as summer ends).

On the other hand, the interiors of continents tend to have the greatest extremes of hot and cold. Even though the Arctic Ocean is farther north than Siberia, the air temperature in Siberia is colder in the winter than the air temperature over the Arctic Ocean. One of the reasons that the southern polar region of Earth is much colder than the northern polar region is that the southern polar region is over a large land area, Antarctica.

If Earth's oceans did not modify climate, we would be subjected to much harsher temperature extremes. Consider the climate of Great Britain. The summers and winters there are generally less severe than those of the northeastern United States. Subzero temperatures are unusual in England. Yet even England, the southernmost part of Great Britain, is farther north than Maine.

What keeps Great Britain from getting so cold? It is the influence of two warm ocean currents called the Gulf Stream and the North Atlantic Current. The Gulf Stream flows past Florida and up the eastern coast of the United States. The North Atlantic Current carries this warm water across the Atlantic to Great Britain. It moderates the temperatures of England, Ireland, Wales, and Scotland.

The oceans have a similar moderating effect on the temperature of our entire planet.

Because the Pacific Ocean is so large, it is one of the keys to the whole world's climate. Meteorologists have even identified a seemingly minor variation in Pacific water temperatures, which every few years, sets off sometimes drastic weather events around the world.

What are other keys to Earth's climate? They are the polar ice caps and the amount of carbon dioxide in the atmosphere.

Everyone has heard of Earth's ice ages—those periods in our world's history when huge sheets of ice called glaciers spread down from polar regions. Scientists do not know exactly what caused the glaciers to form and advance. It is possible that slight variations in Earth's orbit may have played a role.

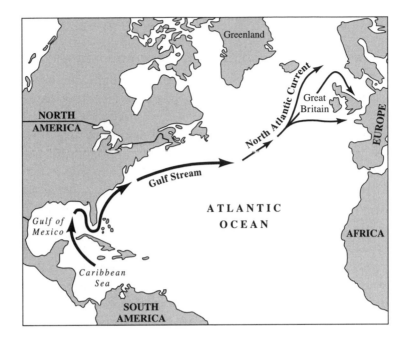

Even though Great Britain is farther north than the northernmost states of the United States, it has much milder weather than Maine, North Dakota, and Montana. Great Britain is warmed by ocean waters carried from the Caribbean Sea and the Gulf of Mexico by the Gulf Stream and the North Atlantic Current.

The distribution of land and ocean in a given era may also encourage glacier formation. As continents move on their various tectonic plates, there may be times when large landmasses cover both polar regions. More land in the polar regions would mean more ice on the surface of Earth. Because ice reflects sunlight, the entire Earth would become colder. If Earth becomes colder, even more ice will form.

What stops and reverses an ice age? As more and more of the world's water freezes, there is less available to absorb carbon dioxide. The amount of carbon dioxide in the atmosphere begins to increase. Because carbon dioxide traps heat, Earth's temperature would also begin to increase. As the temperature increases, the ice would melt and the glaciers would recede.

But there are many other factors that come into play. Earth's climate is very complex. Scientists are beginning to realize that we must avoid doing anything that might disturb the balance of forces that makes Earth's climate what it has been throughout human history. Unfortunately, we appear to have already inadvertently set off an increase in the greenhouse effect. An increase in global temperatures may disrupt the world's climate and agriculture, drown coastal regions, and endanger plants and animals that are already threatened for other reasons.

The Atmosphere of Mars

Mars's atmosphere, like that of Venus, is composed almost entirely of carbon dioxide. But just about everything else about the two atmospheres is radically different.

Mars is too small and too far from the sun to have retained most of its original atmosphere. The atmospheric pressure on Mars is about ninety times less than that on Earth. The pressure varies quite a bit with elevation. It is greatest in valleys like Valles Marineris and least at the tops of volcanoes, which are up to 17 miles (27 km) high.

The atmospheric pressure on Mars also varies seasonally because roughly 20 percent of the planet's entire atmosphere freezes and condenses during the Martian winter. A similar phenomenon may occur on Pluto. (In the case of Pluto, frozen methane apparently clings to the planet during the periods when it is farther from the sun than Neptune is.) On a much larger, more atmospherically active and complex world like Mars, the feat of regularly turning 20 percent of the atmosphere into ground frost is far more remarkable, though.

Remember that this frost is frozen atmosphere. It is composed of frozen carbon dioxide, which is also called dry ice because it has no liquid form. Dry ice freezes at a much lower temperature than ice made from water. (It is often used to simulate smoke or fog in stage productions.)

Because the atmospheric pressure on Mars is much lower than it is on Earth, substances freeze at much lower temperatures. The north pole of Mars reaches a high of about –95°F (–71°C) in the summer, while the south pole rarely gets warmer than –165°F (–109°C). On Mars, water turns to ice at about –95°F (–71°C) and carbon dioxide turns to ice at about –165°F (–109°C). Thus, scientists believe that the Martian north pole is composed primarily of water and that the Martian south pole is composed almost exclusively of carbon dioxide.

There are other differences between the north and south polar ice caps of Mars. These differences provide clues to how the weather of the planet works.

The northern cap reflects much less sunlight than the southern cap. Scientists think that this happens because the northern cap contains more dust (mixed with the ice) than the southern pole. It is summer in the southern hemisphere when Mars is closest to the sun. The sun's heat produces great winds that transport large quantities of dust into the atmosphere. Much of this dust is deposited with the frost condensing at the northern pole (where it is win-

When the carbon dioxide frost which condenses in the Martian
winter is warmed and evaporates, it can leave behind
the incredibly thin layer of water ice we see looking whitish
in this 1979 photograph by the *Viking Lander 2*.

ter). As evidence, some scientists point to the large sand
dunes, the largest in the solar system, in the north polar
region of Mars.

This may not be the answer, however, because over long
periods of time, orbital changes of Mars sometimes lead
one, sometimes the other hemisphere to be the one that
ought to receive the maximum dust in winter. Why are
there not great dune fields in the south, too?

What does exist in both polar regions is the awesome
"layered terrain" of Mars, which is composed of built-up
deposits of dust and ice. This terrain has been called the

"giant's staircases" because it consists of a series of ascending terraces. Each "step" is 30 to 160 feet (9 m to 49 m) tall. Laterally, some run for hundreds of miles.

Mars is also famous for its dust storms, which have been known to spread and shroud the entire planet for several months. Its atmosphere contains large quantities of dust, which produce pink skies and blue sunsets. (A blue sun and blue moon are occasionally seen on Earth when forest fire smoke or desert dust storms are prevalent.)

Mars also has, to judge from the shadows on *Viking Orbiter* photos, storms called *dust devils*. On Earth, these whirlwinds are normally a few hundred to a thousand feet tall. The dust devils of Mars may be up to about 5 miles (8 km) high!

Maximum wind speeds on Mars may reach several hundred miles per hour. Even though the Martian air is so much thinner than ours, these winds still have considerable force.

How could such a cold planet with so little air have such vigorous winds and cyclonic storms? The key is its thin atmosphere. Mars's thinner atmosphere reacts more rapidly to heating or cooling than Earth's. Large temperature differences can create winds, such as those that race madly from the hot, noon end of Valles Marineris to its frigid end, where dawn is just breaking.

The typical diurnal (daily) temperature range of Mars is on the order of 100°F (38°C). The average temperature [–60°F (–51°C)] of Mars is similar to that of a cold day on Antarctica. A typical winter temperature at the poles of Mars is about –240°F (–151°C). The thin atmosphere is so easily heated that, near the equator, noon temperatures may soar as high as 85°F (29°C).

Before you start packing your picnic basket, however, remember the more typical Martian temperatures, the lack of oxygen, the exceeding thinness of the atmosphere, and the complete lack of protection from ultraviolet radiation.

Mars is an astonishingly beautiful wilderness (and one from which we have much to learn), but its beauties are edged with harshness and danger. Our adventurous Mars colonists will learn to love the planet (after learning to respect her). But Mars will be no picnic.

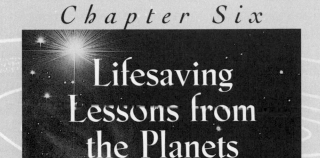

C h a p t e r   S i x

Lifesaving Lessons from the Planets

*N*ot everything we learn from comparing the planets is of immediate practical value. But you can never tell when this information might suggest ways of saving and improving Earth.

For instance, you might suppose that most of the information scientists learn about Earth's plate tectonics by studying other planets would just enter the pages of geology textbooks. In other words, it may be interesting stuff, but it will never prove crucial to human well-being. But consider the fledgling field of earthquake prediction. Some experts think that, with just a little more knowledge, they may be able to predict dangerous quakes more accurately. This knowledge could conceivably come from studies of geological activity on other worlds. (We already have seismographic data for quakes on the moon and Mars.) Planetology might save lives that would otherwise have been lost in cataclysmic earthquakes.

What about the surface of our world? Can other planets tell us anything crucial about that? Consider how many millions of additional people might be fed if scientists understood the processes of wind erosion and soil transport better. Mars could provide an excellent model for such studies.

Think also about the equipment scientists have designed to travel across the incredibly rugged surfaces and harsh environments of other planets. Robot explorers designed to endure the pressure deep within the atmosphere of Venus or Jupiter could be used to explore Earth's oceans. Automated rovers built to survive in the heat of Venus or the cold of Mars should have little trouble crossing Antarctica or entering Earth's volcanoes.

Of course, some of these ideas are highly speculative. The rest of this chapter will highlight two planetary lessons that are much more clear, and are plainly lifesaving. Both of these lessons concern the changes humans are making to Earth's atmosphere.

The atmosphere is essential to our lives. Several minutes without oxygen will kill you. The atmosphere is the place through which you see and hear everything; it is the place through which you communicate with others. The atmosphere is home and life. The most important lessons of planetology may be what our neighbors Venus and Mars can teach us about our own atmosphere and how to preserve it.

Initially Similar Atmospheres

The atmospheres of Venus, Mars, and Earth contain different amounts of the same gases. While carbon dioxide is the major component of Martian and Venusian air, it is a minor constituent of Earth's air. Why the difference?

When the solar system formed, Earth's atmosphere had much more carbon dioxide, Mars had a more substantial atmosphere, and Venus had a shot at producing life. As time passed, Earth produced life, Mars lost most of its atmosphere because it was small and cold, and Venus heated up because it retained too much carbon dioxide in its atmosphere. It is possible that the ocean that may once have covered Venus contained life, but the greenhouse effect caused the planet's temperature to rise. As a result, the ocean dried up and any life-forms it might have contained died.

As you may know from reading about global warming here on Earth, the greenhouse effect is the trapping of heat in a planet's atmosphere by certain gases. These gases permit solar radiation to enter the atmosphere, but prevent infrared (heat) radiation from escaping. They allow solar radiation to get through and warm up the lower atmosphere and surface but then block the escape of infrared (heat) radiation that would otherwise be partly reradiated back out into space.

Mars was simply too small and cold to hold on to most of its atmosphere—even with the help of the most famous of the greenhouse gases, carbon dioxide. Venus was large enough and hot enough to retain its carbon dioxide. Unfortunately, this proved to be a crucial problem to any life that may have been developing there, or that might have developed in later years. The temperature on Venus simply kept rising—by hundreds of degrees Fahrenheit. Any free water and any early life would have succumbed to the tremendous heat.

How did Earth's atmosphere go from one dominated by carbon dioxide to the present one, which consists of nitrogen and oxygen and a relatively small amount of carbon dioxide? To answer this question, we will chronicle the three radically different stages that Earth's atmosphere has passed through in the course of its long history.

Earth, Venus, and Carbon Dioxide

Earth's first atmosphere consisted primarily of the gas from which the solar system formed. Because hydrogen is so lightweight, as time passed, the hydrogen in the original atmosphere began to escape from the gravitational clutch of Earth. Impacts by asteroid-sized bodies may have finished the job more quickly by literally blowing away most of the atmosphere, again and again.

Earth's second atmosphere consisted of carbon dioxide and water vapor—the gases released by its numerous and active volcanoes. Some scientists also think that comet impacts supplied Earth with large quantities of water, and probably some of its carbon dioxide. (This theory writes comets into the script of Earth's history as both villains that crashed and destroyed life and benefactors that supplied the water needed for life.) In any case, approximately 4 billion years ago, Earth began to have an ocean, and above it an atmosphere composed predominantly of carbon dioxide.

Over time, Earth's carbon dioxide atmosphere was changed by the biological processes of the planet's early residents, algae and other very simple plants. As you may know, plants—even one-celled algae—can conduct *photosynthesis*. That is, in the presence of sunlight, they can break down carbon dioxide. They use the carbon and release the other ingredient (oxygen). The transition from an atmosphere composed mostly of carbon dioxide to one that is predominantly nitrogen and oxygen appears to have occurred during the eon from 2 billion to 1 billion years ago.

Earth's carbon dioxide atmosphere must have created a strong greenhouse effect. Why did this effect not heat Earth enough to prevent plants from evolving and covering the planet so that they could eventually decrease the concentration of carbon dioxide in the atmosphere? Why did Earth not become like Venus?

If you guessed that it was because a smaller amount of solar radiation reached the more distant planet Earth, you are right. But a complete explanation of how Earth was able to support early life is more complicated than that.

Have you been wondering why the Venusian atmosphere is so much denser and heavier than Earth's? After all, didn't Earth start out with as much carbon dioxide as Venus, too much for plants to remove by themselves?

Earth and Venus did start out with similar atmospheres, but less solar radiation meant that Earth's oceans did not evaporate away. And that's what made the difference. Even though the amount of volcanic activity on early Venus was probably roughly as great as that on early Earth, the temperature on Venus must have risen a little too high for the water vapor from the volcanoes to condense. As a result, Venus either didn't develop an ocean or lost the one it had by evaporation.

On Earth, the oceans dissolved a great deal of carbon dioxide (they still do) and turned it into carbonic acid, which reacted with rocks and formed carbonates. Today, the total amount of carbon dioxide gas surrounding Venus is about seventy times the amount of air on Earth. But if the carbon dioxide tied up in Earth's carbonate rocks was released into the atmosphere, the amount of carbon dioxide in Earth's atmosphere would be about the same as the amount in Venus's.

So it was really Earth's oceans, and the early plant life in them, that worked together to save each other. They produced an atmosphere that made all oxygen-breathing organisms possible.

Our lesson from Venus is that the amount of carbon dioxide in a planet's atmosphere is a critical factor for that planet's temperature—and for all that depends on temperature and climate.

Humankind turned to the burning of *fossil fuels* to power the new industrial society that emerged fully in the nineteenth century and grew to gargantuan proportions in the twentieth century. Dependence on fossil fuels like oil and coal has produced many regrettable side effects such as air pollution, acid rain, oil spills, and strip mining. Although we cannot yet run our society without fossil fuels, we must make every effort to drastically reduce fossil fuel consumption and develop safe alternative energy sources such as solar power.

Even if we could stop all use of fossil fuels today, it is likely that global warming will be severe enough to affect every life on Earth throughout the twenty-first century. If we consider the fate of Venus, a planet that might have bloomed like Earth and instead turned into a hellish oven of heat, darkness, and acid clouds, we may respond more readily to the danger of increasing the greenhouse effect.

Mars, Earth, and Ozone Depletion

There are many lessons of great importance about how Earth works to learn from studying Mars. While the planet certainly does have its peculiarities, the weather system of Mars is, in general, far simpler than Earth's. Therefore, study of Martian climate and weather may help scientists to better understand Earth's. This knowledge can show humans ways to improve agriculture and prevent loss of life from severe storms. Since the greenhouse effect will probably cause Earth's climate to change radically, anything we can learn from the meteorology of Mars could be helpful.

But there is a simpler and starker message that certain conditions on Mars provide to us, one which we still perhaps need to hear. That message concerns what happens to life on a planet when it loses its protection from ultraviolet radiation.

We do not know if there was ever life on Mars. Scientists were hoping that the *Viking Landers* would find signs of microorganisms in Martian soil samples. At first, the scientists detected some of the chemical changes expected if organisms were present and excitement grew. In the end, *Viking*'s experiments showed that the soil contained no microorganisms. It did not even contain any organic molecules, the so-called "building blocks of life."

It didn't take scientists long to figure out why. The *Viking Orbiters* showed that Mars has no ozone layer—no protection from the sun's ultraviolet radiation. If organic molecules ever existed on Mars, the strong dose of solar UV radiation that reaches the planet's surface must have broken them down. UV radiation has sterilized the surface of Mars. Human activities now threaten Earth's ozone layer. If our planet's protective shield is in danger, so are we.

In 1928, a group of chemists invented a new class of gases called CFCs (chlorofluorocarbons). These gases were eventually used in refrigerators and aerosol spray products. When CFC-containing sprays are sprayed or refrigerators break, these CFCs are released into the atmosphere.

Unlike most compounds, CFCs do not break down easily. They last for years and are carried all the way up to a layer of the atmosphere called the stratosphere. The ozone layer is in the stratosphere.

Ozone is a molecule that contains three oxygen atoms (O_3). It forms when O_2 (oxygen molecules) and O (oxygen atoms) are bombarded with strong UV radiation. Ozone then absorbs UV radiation. As this happens, the ozone splits apart and becomes O_2 and O again. The oxygen molecules and atoms are free to combine into ozone again, and the process continues.

Although CFCs do not react with most molecules, they do react with ozone. A single atom of chlorine from CFCs can destroy thousands of ozone molecules. Fewer ozone molecules means less absorption of UV radiation. If UV radiation is not broken down in the stratosphere, it travels all the way to Earth. Increased exposure to UV radiation can cause skin cancer, eye cataracts, and other medical conditions in humans, as well as other animals.

The first great publicity about the ozone depletion threat hit the newspapers in the United States in the fall of 1974. By 1985, the United States and a few other countries that had already banned using CFCs in aerosols (but not in refrigerators or many other products) asked that all nations agree to the same ban. Many other countries refused.

A few months later, scientists discovered something astonishing: a large hole in the portion of the ozone layer above Antarctica. Since 1985, the hole, which appears when spring returns to the southern hemisphere, has grown larger and larger.

Many politicians and CFC manufacturers dragged their feet. Surely the hole would not expand to reach parts of Australia and South America? It did. Surely ozone levels would not decline significantly in the north temperate zone of Earth where most of the world's population lives? By the early 1990s, they did.

Even though Viking showed us what could happen to a planet without an ozone layer in 1976, our leaders did not pay enough attention.

You can be one of the next generation of leaders who does pay attention. Now you know that planetology is no longer a subject detached from the realities of everyday life—and death—on Earth.

NASA program scientist Robert Watson examines the daily
Total Ozone Mapping Spectrometer (TOMS) data from the
Nimbus-7 satellite. Such efforts are needed to monitor levels
of ozone depletion in Earth's atmosphere.

Chapter Seven

The History of the Solar System

The planets and the sun are not the only bodies in the solar system. There are also four ring systems, dozens of moons, at least tens of thousands of asteroids, probably billions of comets, and truly countless numbers of meteoroids.

Asteroids, comets, and meteoroids are called the "minor members" of the solar system, and sometimes the moons are placed in this category, too. Although these bodies may be minor in size compared to the planets, they are not minor in significance. In fact, understanding where comets come from, and how they ended up where they are today, may be a key to learning how our entire solar system formed.

In this book, we can't possibly profile all the moons of the solar system or even discuss the most important ones in depth. Nor can we study all of the asteroids or comets. We can, however, discuss the minor members in the course of telling a story: a story of how the solar system formed and became the way it now is. Although much of this story is speculation—scientists just don't have enough information yet—it draws upon all of the areas of planetology that have already been discussed in this book.

The Solar Nebula

How did our solar system come into being? There are religious answers to such a question, and they are valid in their own field—the search for spiritual meaning. Here, we are dealing with the scientific answer to the physical formation of the solar system. But you may find your spirit soaring when you hear of some of the grand, majestic, and surprising events that have occurred.

Our scientific story of the solar system begins with the story of our galaxy, a vast rotating spiral of stars, gases, and dust. This mighty and complex structure spins. Its outer regions take hundreds of millions of years to complete one full circle. As it spins, its mass is constantly redistributed. This gives rise to density waves. These density waves push on the gas and dust, so that some regions have higher concentrations of these materials than other regions. Scientists theorize that these waves may cause a particular *nebula* (a cloud of gas and dust in space) to become so concentrated that its gravity begins to make it contract. If the nebula contracts enough, its center will experience such intense pressure that it becomes a star.

Imagine the nebula that may have formed our sun and solar system about 5 billion years ago. At first, this solar nebula was visible only by virtue of any nearby stars shining on it, or because it blocked out the view of stars beyond it. But as it contracted, its central region became denser and denser. The pressure of the outlying layers pushing on it increased its temperature. Eventually, the pressure and temperature at the center of the nebula reached a critical point, and a nuclear fusion reaction occurred and was sus-

New stars and possibly new solar systems are being
formed in the giant cloud of interstellar gas and dust
known as the Orion Nebula.

tained. (The hydrogen atoms at the center of the nebula had been pressed together until they fused, forming helium and giving off enormous amounts of energy.) Our sun had been born.

As the young sun rotated, the rest of the nebula formed a flattened disk in the equatorial plane of the sun. This is the disk from which the planets eventually formed. In space, when small bodies such as gas molecules, atoms, and grains of dust orbit a larger one, they often form the shape of a flattened disk. One example within our solar system is the rings surrounding Saturn (and other planets). The ice particles in these rings are confined to orbiting Saturn in a thin, flat disk in the equatorial plane of Saturn.

Dust grains in the solar nebula began to collide with each other. Because most were headed in pretty much the same direction and were traveling at similar speed, the collisions between dust particles were often gentle enough for them to stick together. This process, by which increasingly larger bodies were formed, is called *accretion*. The bodies formed by accretion are called *planetesimals*. All of the original planetesimals had the potential to become part of a planet. As you will see later, not all did.

When a planetesimal became large enough its increased gravity allowed it to sweep up smaller ones much more easily. As a result, a few planetesimals became much larger than all the others. Eventually, these planetisimals became planets.

In some cases, two or more planetisimals competed for their planetary status. But the battle was not easy. For instance, we now believe that it was a planetesimal perhaps roughly the size of Mars (more than 4,000 miles, or 6,000 km, wide) that smashed into the forming Earth when it was nearing its present size (slightly less than 8,000 miles, or 13,000 km, in diameter). Earth survived this glancing blow, and a large part of the planetesimal's molten substance produced during the collision was used to seal Earth's wounds.

The rest of the planetesimal's fragments began to orbit Earth. These fragments joined together into a single body: the moon. At this point the moon was very close to Earth. Tidal forces between Earth and the moon pushed the moon into an ever larger orbit and slowed Earth's spin. This process continues, although extremely slowly. As a result, the length of an Earth day is increasing.

Worlds of Rock and Ice

Eventually the largest planetesimals were able to alter the paths of the smaller ones. As a result, the smaller planetesimals sometimes approached the larger ones from different directions and collisions were stronger.

By now, the small planetesimals had cooled enough to be entirely solid. As they collided, they broke into many pieces. Eventually, they became countless small bits of rock and iron scattered throughout the solar system (perhaps especially the inner solar system). They became meteoroids. Today, meteoroids may also come from the tails of comets and from asteroid collisions that occurred later in the history of the solar system.

The large planetisimals forming close to the young sun were very different from those forming farther out. In the inner regions of the solar nebula, temperatures were higher and only metallic and silicate (rocky) particles could condense. Therefore, the planetisimals—and eventually the planets of the inner solar system—were dominated by metal and rock.

In the outer solar system, rock and metal combined with ice to form much larger bodies. Because these planetisimals had a great deal of mass and strong gravitational fields, they were able to retain hydrogen in their atmospheres. As a result, they eventually became truly gigantic.

Many of the moons of the gas giants contain large amounts of ice. Some of these worlds contain as much or even more ice than rock. The ice-to-rock ratio of a particular moon can be calculated based on its density. (Ice is far less dense than rock.) Density can be calculated using information about the moon's size (from *Voyager* photos) and mass (from orbital studies).

Scientists expected that the four big Galilean moons of Jupiter would be like a miniature solar system. In other words, the moons closer to the heat of young Jupiter would have a higher proportion of rock-to-ice than the outer bodies. The Voyagers proved that this was true. Io, the innermost big moon, contained the highest percentage of rock, and Callisto, the outermost big moon, contained the lowest percentage of rock.

The rule that worlds of the inner solar system are predominantly rock and metal while those of the outer solar system are icy is borne out not only by the planets and moons, but also by two other classes of objects: asteroids and comets.

Asteroids are made of rock and iron. Most are located in an asteroid belt located at the outer edge of the zone of the terrestrial planets. Comets are made of ice and dust. Some may have rocky cores. Most comets may have originally come from just beyond the orbital zone of the gas giants. Could it be that asteroids are the rocky planetesimals and comets are the icy planetesimals that were never swept up by the larger planetesimals?

Both comets and asteroids can be sources of meteoroids, and some of the objects that scientists originally thought were asteroids are probably the rocky cores of

As the *Galileo* spacecraft zoomed by Earth in December of 1992, it took this magnificent shot of our planet and moon.

inactive or "dead" (their ice is used up) comets. But there are other mysteries about comets and asteroids.

Why didn't the asteroids join together to form a single planet? Jupiter's mighty gravitational influence may have swept up or away so much material from this region that there wasn't enough left to form a full-sized planet. It is also possible that the thousands of asteroids in the asteroid belt today are pieces of a few larger bodies. The surface cratering of Gaspra and Ida (photographed by the *Galileo* spacecraft) suggest that these asteroids are only a few hundred million and a billion years old, respectively. Since the solar system is more than 4 billion years old, both of these asteroids must truly be "chips off the old block" (that is, pieces of earlier, larger asteroids). How have asteroids in the asteroid belt escaped to pass across the orbits of Earth, Venus, and even Mercury? Through the tiny instability in their orbits, which can be predicted by the strange new science of "chaos."

All of these questions about asteroids require more study. But our uncertainties about asteroids seem small compared to what we don't know about comets.

Where Do Comets Come From?

If we return to our story of how the solar system developed, we next have to note that in the final days that Earth was growing, there came to it a source of water: bombardment by comets. This was perhaps not Earth's only source of water, but possibly an important one.

Before revealing where scientists think these comets came from and why they suddenly started bombarding Earth, we need to discuss what comets are and where they come from at present.

Comets are the most mysterious class of object in the solar system. Some scientists believe that they have changed very little over the billions of years that the solar system has existed. As long as a comet is far from the sun, it consists of nothing more than dusty (and often dark-surfaced) ice. Most of the ice is frozen water, but some is frozen carbon dioxide, carbon monoxide, and other chemicals. This chunk of ice is called the nucleus of the comet. Some comet nuclei are very large (about 10 miles, or 16 km,

wide), while others are relatively small (less than 1 mile, or 1.6 km, wide).

As a comet nucleus approaches the Sun, its ice begins to *sublime* (go straight from ice to gas). As the ice turns to gas, dust particles within the nucleus rush out, producing a vast cloud around the nucleus. This cloud is called the *coma* (from the Latin word for "hair" because of its fuzzy appearance). The coma may be larger than hundreds of thousands of miles across. Together, the nucleus and the coma that surrounds it are known as the *head* of the comet.

Often a streamer or fan of gas and/or dust is pushed out from the coma in the direction opposite from the sun by the pressure of solar radiation and the solar wind. Such an extension from the comet may stretch out tens of millions of miles. This *tail* may be incredibly long, but it contains so little material that you could condense it and keep it in an auditorium.

Comets shine partly by reflecting sunlight and partly by emitting light of their own. The emitted light is mostly a result of ionization, which occurs when some of the comet's atoms and molecules are struck by the particles of the solar wind.

Almost all comets have highly elongated orbits around the sun. These orbits are shaped more like cigars than circles. This means that for only part of each orbit (usually a very small part) is a comet close enough to the sun for a coma to form. For many comets, the coma forms when the

A *Voyager* montage shows Jupiter and its four big Galilean satellites: Io (far left), Europa (in front of Jupiter), Ganymede (left foreground), and Callisto (lower right corner).

The mosaic of the asteroid 243 Ida was created with five photographs taken by *Galileo* when it was about 2,000 miles (3,200 km) away from the asteroid. Ida measures about 32 miles (52 km) in length.

comet is about the same distance from the sun as Mars is. The rest of the time the comet is somewhere out in the outer solar system. It is nothing but a 1 to 10 mile (2 to 16 km) wide chunk of special ice. It is too small to reflect much light and, therefore, very difficult to detect from Earth.

How far out into the outer solar system do comets go? The answer depends on the comet. Some comets, called *periodic comets* (or short-period comets) circle the sun in less than 200 years.

Most periodic comets complete one revolution in less than 100 years. One of the best-known comets, Comet Halley, passes by Earth once every 75 or so years as it approaches the part of its orbit closest to the sun.

The *aphelion* (an orbit's farthest point from the sun) of comets with periods of less than 20 years is close to the orbit of Jupiter. Close encounters with Jupiter must have altered the orbits of these comets. These comets are said to belong to "Jupiter's family of comets." The other gas giants may also have their own—though much smaller—families of comets.

Long-period comets have periods of more than 200 years. Most have periods of thousands or millions of years. These comets have extremely elongated elliptical orbits. The aphelion of such a comet is far beyond that of any of the planets.

The Oort Cloud

Scientists believe that when the solar system was created, there was only one type of comet—long-period comets. Because the aphelia of many periodic comets are so close to the orbit of Jupiter, that planet's powerful gravitational pull probably altered the course of the comets as they passed close to it.

Each time a comet passes by the planets, it faces the danger of being pulled out of its orbit by the gravitational pull of Jupiter (or possibly other gas giants). If the comet's orbit is shortened, it will be exposed more frequently to the sun's heat. Each time the comet approaches the sun, more of the ice in its nucleus will turn to vapor. As a result,

This 8-minute exposure of Comet Bennett was
taken on April 16, 1970.

short-period comets eventually die out. Scientists have
even seen some comets die.

Scientists now believe that the gas giants must capture
new comets all the time because many of the periodic
comets that we see are too bright to have circled the sun
every 100 years since the solar system formed. There must
be a source of fresh comet nuclei somewhere farther from
the sun.

In 1950, astronomer Jan Oort proposed that there is a
vast cloud containing billions of comet nuclei far beyond
the orbit of Pluto. This cloud may surround the parts of the
solar system like a protective shell. Because so many long-
period comets have periods of millions of years, their aphe-

lion—presumably, in the *Oort Cloud*—may be halfway to the nearest star.

The Oort Cloud is anything but dense. The cloud is so large and the nuclei are so small that there is very little chance of the nuclei colliding.

Once scientists accepted the theory of an Oort Cloud, a new question arose. How could the comet nuclei, orbiting the sun way out in the Oort Cloud, ever get into new, extremely elongated orbits that come cruising by the planets as they move toward the sun? What causes the comet nuclei in the Oort Cloud to become long-period comets? The answer might have something to do with another star.

As the sun and solar system orbit around the center of our galaxy—the Milky Way galaxy—there must be times when the solar system passes closer than usual to another star. When this happens, some of nuclei in the Oort Cloud speed up, and fly right out of the solar system. Other nuclei slow down, and fall inward toward the sun.

Although the comet will return to the Oort Cloud after passing the sun, it has become locked into a new, highly elongated orbit. Its aphelion is in the Oort Cloud, but its perihelion is near the sun.

It will take different amounts of time for each of the nuclei displaced by the passing star to reach the inner solar system. The last of these new comets may pass by Earth a million years after our solar system passed unusually close to a star. By that time, the solar system may have passed yet another star, causing the whole process to begin again.

Although the idea of an Oort Cloud is astonishing, apparently, it is basically correct. Since 1950, scientists have revised Oort's original theory somewhat.

The basic theory of the Oort Cloud cannot, however, explain how the untold billions of comets ended up in the Oort Cloud in the first place. You see, scientists believe

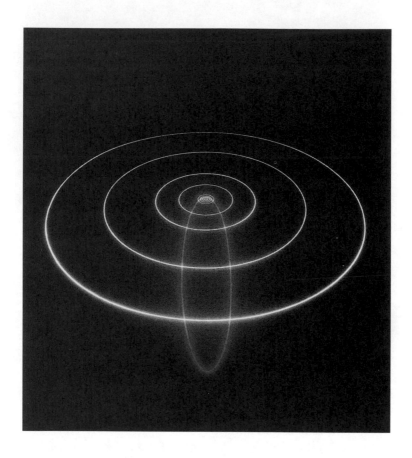

The highly elliptical orbit of Halley's Comet is shown in
relation to the more circular orbits of the eight planets
from Mercury out to Neptune.

that comets could not have formed at temperatures as low
as those that exist at the Oort Cloud's distance from the
sun. They believe that they formed at the same distance
from the sun as the outer gas giants.

You have already learned that the gravity of the large

planetisimals altered the paths of the smaller ones. The gravity of the gas giants threw the icy planetesimals—the comets—into wild orbits. Billions of comets were whisked in all directions. Some hit the gas giants (and were easily absorbed). Others escaped from the solar system altogether. But most were tossed out to the solar system's outermost regions, where they formed the Oort Cloud.

Millions of the icy planetisimals were also flung toward the terrestrial planets. As a result, the early Earth was bombarded by comets. Many scientists believe that these comets helped form Earth's early oceans. Comets may have also brought organic molecules—the building blocks of life—to our planet.

The Kuiper Belt

There is one last important twist to the story of comets that should be mentioned.

In the 1980s, a team of scientists calculated that short-period comets could not be derived from the long-period comets that had originally come from the Oort Cloud. The reason had something to do with the way the comets orbit.

Short-period comets orbit close to the plane of the planets' orbits, whereas long-period comets come in at all inclinations (from all parts of the spherical Oort Cloud). Scientists concluded that there was no easy way to get the long-period Oort comets from highly inclined (tilted) orbits into such flattened orbits.

The picture that has emerged is of an outer Oort Cloud, an inner Oort Cloud, and a *Kuiper Belt* (named after twentieth-century American astronomer Gerard P. Kuiper, who first proposed it in 1951). According to current theory, the inner Oort Cloud is far more dense with comets than the outer cloud, and perhaps somewhat more flattened, merging into the Kuiper Belt, which would be even more flattened—truly a belt, an extension of the plane in which the planets generally revolve around the sun. Short-period comets appear to be escapees from the Kuiper Belt, while long-period comets are escapees from the Oort Cloud.

Is there a Kuiper Belt? Scientists weren't sure until the early 1990s. That's when they began to discover an increasing number of mysterious objects that traveled in circular orbits around the sun at the distances of Uranus, Neptune, and even a bit beyond Pluto.

Scientists initially thought that these objects—and similar ones closer to the sun, including one named Chiron—were asteroids. Chiron was discovered between the orbits of Saturn and Uranus in 1977. Because it was at least 100 miles (160 km) wide and showed no trace of a coma, scientists didn't think that it could possibly be a comet nucleus.

In the late 1980s, as Chiron approached its perihelion, it began to form a coma. Chiron was a comet—a very, very big comet. During the 1990s, scientists have discovered a number of small objects in the outer solar system. There is now strong evidence that these objects are comets. They may be some of the closest and largest members of the Kuiper Belt.

Is It a Comet?

The idea of essentially rocky bodies forming in the inner regions of the solar nebula and predominantly icy bodies in the outer regions are supported by scientists' findings. Thus, Pluto and its moon Charon, the object Chiron, and perhaps some moons of the outer planets may all be planetesimals left over from the formation of the solar system.

Does this mean that Pluto is really a comet? No, at least a few of the remaining planetesimals in the outer solar system were large enough and contained enough rock to be something other than a comet. Still, it is interesting to ponder what the dividing line between a very rocky, dusty comet and a very icy moon, asteroid, or planet is. Are there celestial bodies with characteristics of both?

The Finishing Touches

Trying to unravel the mysteries of comets took us away from chronicling the history of the solar system. But this digression was fascinating—and necessary. We can see now that the theory of the solar nebula forming planets through accretion of planetesimals helped us understand the great mysteries of comets. We can also see the importance of scientists studying comets further. Hopefully, they will eventually be able to obtain samples of a fresh comet, which should be more pristine (unchanged since the days of the early solar system) than any of the meteorites scientists have collected. Such samples would provide more detailed information about the solar nebula and the early days of our solar system.

What else needs to be said about the development of Earth, the other planets, and the solar system after the bombardment of the inner solar system by comets?

The last powerful impacts by large rocky planetesimals can explain the varying tilts of the planets as they spin. Originally, the planets all spun upright and in the same direction as the spin of the solar nebula. A massive world like Jupiter was not affected by impacts. As a result, its tilt remained virtually unchanged.

For Uranus, the final impact was powerful enough to knock the planet over on its side. Scientists believe that the strength of the impact was magnified significantly by the direction of the blow.

This montage of photos taken by *Voyager* shows Saturn
and six of its eighteen (or more) moons.

Most planets, including Earth, have a moderate tilt relative to their rotational axis. Even though the impact that
gave birth to our planet's moon was the result of a collision
with a huge planetisimal, Earth was not knocked over
because the glancing blow came from a direction similar to
that from which Earth was spinning.

Of course, far lesser impacts by asteroids or comets have continued to have important effects on planets throughout the history of the solar system—especially on a planet whose surface has a delicate bloom of something fragile called life. The asteroid or comet impact that apparently killed off the dinosaurs also annihilated a majority of the other species on Earth.

We've offered explanations for moons (the big ones of the gas giants formed with their planets like secondary planets; the smaller moons were captured planetesimals). We've also offered explanations for asteroids, comets, and meteoroids. But just to remind you that our explanations are far from complete, that this story of the solar system's origin and life is still unverified and questionable in many ways, take a look at a photograph or through a small telescope at the rings of Saturn.

The rings of Saturn are arguably the most spectacular and the most beautiful sight in our solar system. Yet scientists know relatively little about them or the rings around other planets. While Saturn's rings are made of reflective ice, those of Neptune and Uranus consist of dark dust.

What causes all the intricate structure of Saturn's rings? Why have different kinds of rings formed around the different planets? How enduring are planetary rings? How did the rings form? Scientists just don't know.

Perhaps you will become a planetary scientist and help discover some of the answers.

Chapter Eight

The Future

*W*hat does the future hold for our solar system? And what does the future hold for planetology and those who wish to study this exciting field? The answers are connected. Our exploratory missions will probably provide a second golden age of knowledge and adventure for planetary scientists. This second golden age may be many times richer than the first.

Our missions are also likely to make changes to the surfaces of some worlds. What kinds of changes will we make to other planets? If we are wise, they will be careful and gentle ones. Bases on the moon, colonies on Mars, mines on asteroids—all are possibilities that should be explored, but only with great care. You have learned about the dangerous changes that human society has wrought—often recklessly, often for greedy and shortsighted purposes—to Earth's environment. The planets offer us a chance to do better, to have learned our lesson—or to reenact thoughtlessness and tragedy.

There have been proposals for *terraforming* (making more Earthlike) other planets. Is this wise? Until scientists can rule out the possibility of any native Martian life, we should absolutely not alter large parts of Mars's environment to suit our liking. Although it may take years or even decades to figure out the best way to make Mars habitable, it is not too early to discuss the ethics of terraforming and any other changes caused by our exploration of the moon, Mars, and other bodies in space.

Isn't it ironic that some of us are thinking about terraforming when we have already inadvertently begun changing our own precious planet into something slightly but nevertheless dangerously more like Venus and Mars? The greenhouse effect and global warming, the ozone layer and ozone depletion—these are the ways that we have changed our own planet. Shouldn't we worry about how we are making our own planet unlivable before we worry about how we can make other worlds more livable?

If we show concerns and renewed respect for our Earth—and for all planetary environments—as we explore space, the future can be bright. During the last few years of the century, scientists will interpret photographs and data collected by the *Galileo* spacecraft and other unmanned missions. Some of these missions may include landers that rove around and perhaps even bring back soil samples. The years beyond should feature similar missions to other worlds, a base on the moon, and perhaps even humans on Mars.

You may become involved with these adventures. They could actually be organized and carried out so wisely that they set good examples for taking care of our own planet. A mission to Mars, with male and female astronauts from many countries, could also be wondrous enough to capture humanity's imagination and help bring us together.

Studying other planets helps us learn about our own world. Perhaps visiting other planets will help us find our own.

APPENDIX

TABLE 1

Planet	Rotation Period	Axis Tilt (to orbital plane)	Distance from Sun (millions of km)	Orbital Period
Mercury	58.65 Earth days	0°	57.9	87.97 Earth days
Venus	243.01 Earth days (retrograde)	117° 18'	108.2	224.7 Earth days
Earth	23 h 56 min 4.1 s	23° 27'	149.6	365.26 Earth days
Mars	24 h 37 min 22.6 s	25° 12'	227.9	686.98 Earth days
Jupiter	9 h 50.5 min	3° 07'	778.4	11.86 Earth years
Saturn	0 h 14 min	26° 44'	1,424	29.46 Earth years
Uranus	17 h 14 min (retrograde)	97° 52'	2,872	84.01 Earth years
Neptune	16 h 3 min	29° 34'	4,499	64.8 Earth years
Pluto	6.39 Earth days (retrograde)	98°	5,943	248.6 Earth years

TABLE 2

Planet	Average Radius (km)	Temperature (°K)	Mass (relative to Earth)	Density (kg/m³)	Surface Gravity (relative to Earth)
Mercury	2,439	100–700	0.0562	5,430	0.38
Venus	6,052	700	0.815	5,240	0.91
Earth	6,378	250–300	1.0	5,520	1.00
Mars	3,397	210–300	0.1074	3,940	0.39
Jupiter	71,492	110–150	317.9	1,330	2.54
Saturn	60,268	95	95.1	690	1.07
Uranus	25,559	58	14.56	1,270	0.90
Neptune	25,269	56	17.24	1,640	1.14
Pluto	1,140	40	0.0018	2,100	0.06

TABLE 3

Planet	Gases in Atmosphere (in order of relative abundance)
Mercury	Very small amounts of sodium, potassium, helium, hydrogen
Venus	Carbon dioxide, carbon monoxide, hydrogen chloride, hydrogen fluoride, water, argon, nitrogen, oxygen, hydrogen sulfide, sulfur dioxide, helium
Earth	Nitrogen, oxygen, water, argon, carbon dioxide, neon, helium, methane, krypton, nitrous oxide, ozone, xenon, hydrogen, radon
Mars	Carbon dioxide, carbon monoxide, water, oxygen, ozone, argon, nitrogen
Jupiter	Hydrogen, helium, methane, ammonia, water, carbon monoxide, acetylene, ethane, phosphine, germane
Saturn	Hydrogen, helium, methane, ammonia, acetylene, ethane, phosphine, propane
Uranus	Hydrogen, helium, methane
Neptune	Hydrogen, helium, methane, ethane
Pluto	Methane

TABLE 4

Planet	Number of Satellites	Names of Satellites
Mercury	None	
Venus	None	
Earth	1	Moon
Mars	2	Phobos, Deimos
Jupiter	16	Metis, Adrastea, Amalthea, Thebe, Io Europa, Ganymede, Callisto, Leda, Himalia, Lysithea, Elara, Ananke, Carme, Pasiphae
Saturn	18	Pan, Atlas, Prometheus, Pandora, Epimetheus, Janus, Mimas, Enceladus, Tethys, Telesto, Calypso, Dione, Helene, Rhea, Titan, Hyperion, Iapetus, Phoebe
Uranus	15	Cordelia, Ophelia, Bianca, Cressida, Desdemona, Juliet, Portia, Rosalind, Belinda, Puck, Miranda, Ariel, Umbriel, Titania, Oberon
Neptune	8	Naiad, Thalassa, Despina, Galatea, Larissa, Proteus, Triton, Nereid
Pluto	1	Charon

GLOSSARY

accretion—growth by a clumping together of smaller bodies, the way scientists believe the planets formed.

aphelion—the far point of an orbit around the sun.

asteroid—a rocky world smaller than a planet but larger than a meteoroid (larger than about a few hundred feet across), in many cases found between the orbits of Mars and Jupiter (the "asteroid belt"). Asteroids are also known as "minor planets."

asteroid belt—a region between Mars and Jupiter in which thousands of asteroids orbit.

atmosphere—the gaseous layer surrounding a planet's solid core and/or liquid part.

aurora—also known as "the Northern Lights" or "aurora borealis" in the northern hemisphere and "aurora australis" in the southern hemisphere. The aurora is glowing rays, patches, and sheets concentrated in the skies around Earth's (or another planet's) polar regions. It is caused by upper atmosphere gases being energized by solar particles trapped and accelerated in the planet's magnetosphere.

chlorofluorocarbon (CFC)—a class of chemicals used in aerosol sprays and refrigerants that has been destroying parts of Earth's protective ozone layer.

coma (of a comet)—the cloud of gas and dust that forms around a comet's icy "nucleus" when it is heated enough by the sun.

comet—a mass of dusty ices (frozen water, carbon monoxide, carbon dioxide, and other chemicals) usually about 1 to 10 miles (1.6 to 16 km) in diameter which when exposed to enough solar radiation develops a "coma" around its icy "nucleus." Coma and nucleus together make up the "head" of the comet, and if solar radiation pressure and the solar wind push out enough dust and gas from the head they form into a "tail" of the comet.

Copernican system—a system in which the planets circle the sun (a heliocentric system) proposed in modern times by Nicholas Copernicus.

deuterium—a form of hydrogen.

double star system—a solar system that has two suns.

dust devil—a whirlwind caused by certain kinds of local heating effects.

Earth day—24 hours; the length of a day on Earth. the length of a day is different on every planet. It is determined by the time it takes for the planet to complete one rotation.

ellipse—a closed curve that is more elongated than a circle.

epicycle—extra circular motions that planets were required to follow in different versions of the incorrect Ptolemaic system.

flyby—a spacecraft encounter with a planet or other solar system body in which the craft merely passes by, without assuming orbit around the body or landing on it.

fossil fuel—a fuel such as oil, coal, or natural gas that is formed as plant and animal materials decay.

gas giant—a planet in which gaseous outer layers form a large percentage of the planet's bulk (Jupiter, Saturn, Uranus, Neptune).

geocentric—Earth-centered.

global warming—a theory that claims that the average temperature of the Earth is increasing due to an increase in the amount of carbon dioxide and other gases released into the atmosphere by certain human activities, especially the burning of fossil fuels.

greenhouse effect—the tendency of carbon dioxide and some other gases to trap heat and therefore raise the temperature of an atmosphere and produce global warming.

head (of a comet)—the combined nucleus and coma of a comet.

heliocentric—sun-centered.

hydrosphere—the liquid layer on Earth's surface.

inferior planet—planets that are closer to the sun than Earth is (Mercury and Venus).

Jovian planet—a planet like Jupiter (Jove) in structure and composition (see gas giant).

Kuiper Belt—a belt of comets believed to exist out at and somewhat beyond the orbits of the outermost known planets.

lithosphere—the solid or rock part of a planet.

long-period comet—a comet that orbits the sun in more than 200 years, thought to be derived from the Oort Cloud.

magnetosphere—the area of space around some planets in which the planet's magnetic field predominates over the direct flow of the "solar wind" but contains trapped particles from that wind.

mantle—the layer of the Earth between the outer crust and inner core.

meteor—the streak of light that occurs when a meteoroid hits a planet's atmosphere.

meteorite—a meteoroid that falls through the atmosphere and strikes the surface of a planet.

meteoroid—a rocky body in space smaller than an asteroid (say, no more than a few hundred feet in diameter). If seen burning up in Earth's atmosphere, it is called a meteor (sometimes it is called a shooting star or falling star). If a meteroid hits the ground, it is called a meteorite.

nebula—a cloud of gas and dust at whose contracting center the sun formed and in whose surrounding regions the planets and other bodies of the solar system began to condense.

nucleus (of a comet)—the solid central mass of a comet.

Oort Cloud—the vast swarm of pristine comets which extends from far beyond Pluto outward nearly to other solar systems.

ozone layer—the region of Earth's atmosphere from about 10 to 30 miles (16 to 48 km) up that contains the largest percentages of ozone and protects the Earth's surface from excessive levels of damaging ultraviolet radiation from the sun.

perihelion—the near point of an orbit around the sun.

periodic comet—a comet with an orbital period around the sun of 200 years or less, thought to be derived from the Kuiper Belt. (Also called short-period comet.)

photosynthesis—the process in which a plant converts carbon dioxide and water to oxygen and glucose.

planet—a large body (much larger than the largest asteroid) orbiting independently around a sun.

planetesimal—a rocky or icy body common in the earliest days of the solar system which in many cases clumped together by "accretion" to form the planets.

120

planetology—study of the planets, but (at least for our purposes here) with added emphasis on comparison of the planets and the systems they all have in common.

plate tectonics—the geological phenomenon in which discrete sections of a world's crust undergo movement and interactions with each other.

Ptolemaic system—the incorrect geocentric (Earth-centered) system popularized by Ptolemy and believed for over a thousand years until Copernicus proved it was wrong.

retrograde motion—the seemingly backward (westward) motion of planets in relation to the stars that occurs for a while when Earth is passing them (or, in the case of the faster planets Mercury and Venus, when they are passing Earth).

satellite—if natural, a moon; if artificial, a human-made object launched into an orbit around Earth or another body in space.

seismograph—a device used to measure and record a planet's interior vibrations.

shepherd satellite—moons to either side of a planetary ring whose gravitational influence keeps the particles of the ring concentrated.

shield volcano—a broad rounded volcano that is built up by successive outpourings of very fluid lava.

solar flare—disruptions on the sun that eject huge quantities of atomic particles out into space, and may eventually lead to aurora displays.

solar system— the system formed by a sun (star) and whatever planets, moons, asteroids, comets, meteoroids, and other objects are under its gravitational control.

solar wind—the ceaseless outward flow of atomic particles in a plasma from the sun.

spectroscopy—the process or technique of investigating the components of the electromagnetic spectrum emitted by an object.

stratosphere—the part of Earth's atmosphere that extends from about 7 miles (11 km) to 31 miles (50 km) above the planet's surface.

sublime—to change directly from a solid to a gas.

superior planet—a planet that is more distant from the sun than Earth is (Mars, Jupiter, Saturn, Neptune, Uranus, Pluto).

tail (of a comet)—the streak or fan of gas and dust pushed away from a comet's coma by the solar wind and radiation pressure when the comet is near the sun.

terraforming—the altering of conditions on another world to make them more closely resemble those on Earth.

terrestrial planet—a planet with rocky bodies and comparatively thin layers of surrounding atmosphere (Earth, Venus, Mars, and Mercury).

thermonuclear reaction—a chemical reaction in which hydrogen nuclei combine and enormous quantities of energy are released.

Van Allen Belts—three belts of radiation that surround Earth.

zodiac—the band of constellations in the sky in which the sun, moon, and planets are always located.

FOR FURTHER READING

Books

Beatty, J., et al. *The New Solar System,* 3rd ed. Boston. Sky Publishing and Cambridge University Press, 1990.

Hartmann, W., and R. Miller. *The History of Earth.* New York: Workman, 1993.

Littmann, M. *Planets Beyond: The Outer Solar System,* 2nd ed. New York: Wiley, 1990.

Miles F., and N. Booth. *Race to Mars.* New York: Harper and Row, 1988.

Miller R. and W. Hartmann. *The Grand Tour: A Traveler's Guide to the Solar System.* New York: Workman, 1993.

Sagan, C. *Pale Blue Dot.* New York: Random House, 1994.

Schaaf, F. *Seeing the Solar System.* New York: Wiley, 1991.

Magazines

Astronomy. Kalmbach Publishing, P.O. Box 1612, Waukesha, WI 53187.

Sky & Telescope. P.O. Box 9111, Belmont, MA 02178.

The Planetary Report. The Planetary Society, 65 N. Catlina Ave., Pasadena, CA 91106.

INDEX

ABOUT THE AUTHOR

Fred Schaaf writes the popular monthly "Stars and Planets" column in *Sky and Telescope* magazine and an almanac column on astronomy, weather, and other topics for *Mother Earth News*. He has also written a weekly column in the Atlantic City newspaper *The Press* for more than 20 years. His work has appeared in *Highlights for Children*, *Boys' Life*, *Omni*, and *Astronomy*. Mr. Schaaf drafted the original version of a state of New Jersey law to study light pollution. He lives on the edge of the Pine Barrens in the southern part of the state, and is currently working on his eleventh book about astronomy.